With Hand and Heart

With Hand and Heart

The Courtship Letters of
FRANKLIN B. HOUGH and MARIAH KILHAM
January through May
1849

Vivian G. Smith, Editor

Rhonda Ortlieb, Artist

Lewis County Historical Society
Lyons Falls, New York

North Country Books, Inc.
Utica, New York

With Hand and Heart

ISBN 978-0-925168-03-0

Library of Congress Cataloging-in-Publication Data

Hough, Franklin Benjamin, 1822-1885.
With hand and heart : the courtship letters of Franklin B. Hough and Mariah Kilham, January through May, 1849 / Vivian G. Smith, editor ; art work by Rhonda Ortlieb.
p. cm.
ISBN 978-0-925168-03-0 (pbk.) :
1. Hough, Franklin Benjamin, 1922-1885—Correspondence. 2. Kilham, Mariah, b. ca. 1828—Correspondence. 3. New York (State)—Biography. 4. Courtship—New York (State)—History—19th century. I. Kilham, Mariah, b. ca. 1828. II. Smith, Vivian G. III. Title.
CT275.H64713A4 1993
974.7'03'092—dc20 93-21786
CIP

Published by
North Country Books, Inc.
18 Irving Place
Utica, New York 13501-5618

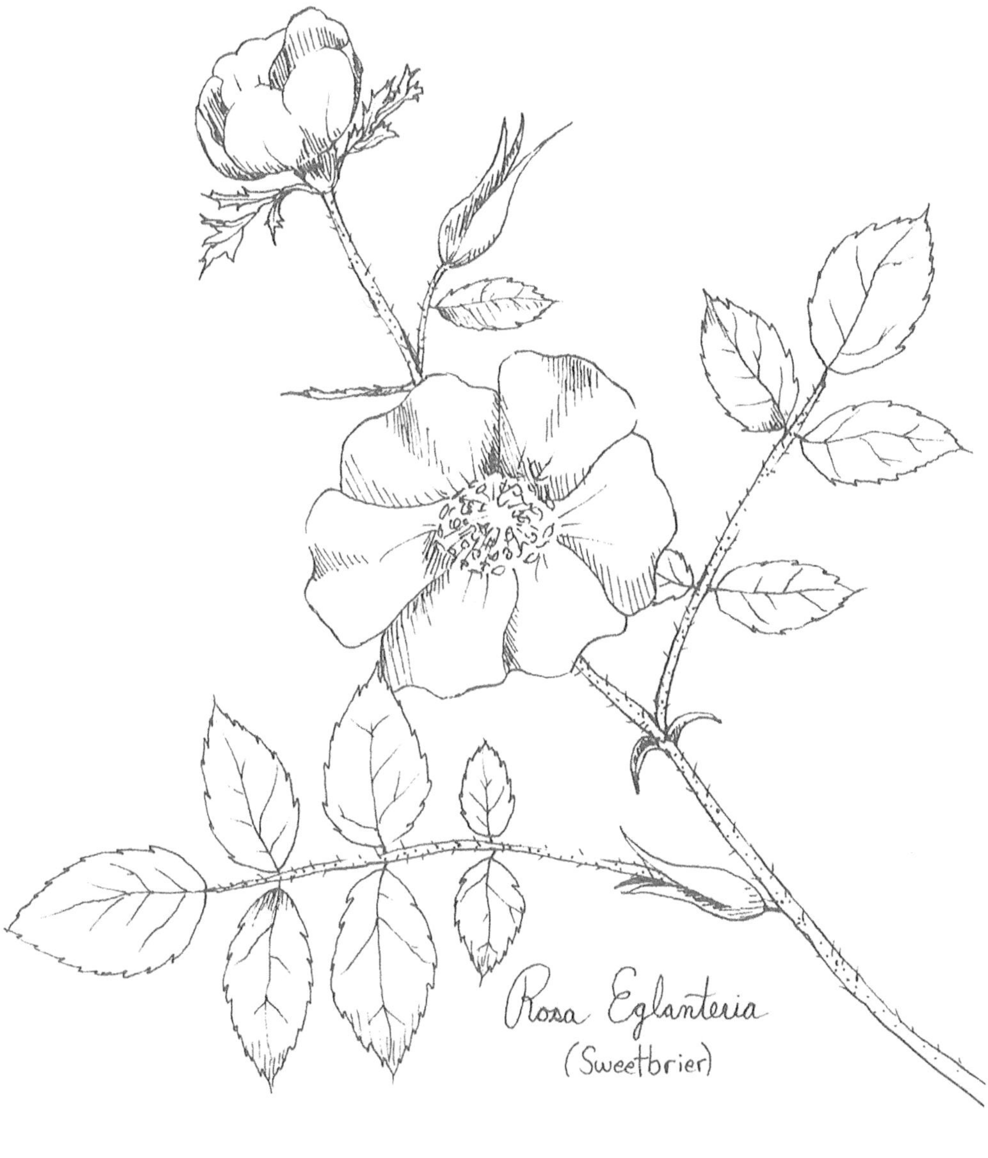
Rosa Eglanteria
(Sweetbrier)

Dedication

To the late
Dorothy Patricia Hough (1920-1985)
great-granddaughter of Franklin and Mariah
whose generosity to this Society has made
great things possible.

Table of Contents

Frontispiece v

Dedication vii

List of Illustrations xi

Introduction xiii

Acknowledgments xv

Preface xvii

Biography of Franklin B. Hough by Edith Pilcher 1

The Kilham Family 5

The Letters 7

Postscript 123

Illustrations

Frontispiece, *Rosa eglanteria* (Sweetbrier Rose) v

Engraving of Franklin in his later years xix

Claytonia virginica (Spring Beauty) 16

Mariah's letter, February 4 20

Paeonia (Peony) 23

Mailing side of the letter from Franklin, February 9 28

Hepatica americana (Round-lobed Hepatica) 30

The maze letter from Franklin, March 1 46

Trillium erectum (Red Trillium, Wake Robin) 49

Mariah's letter, March 4 53

Franklin's letter, March 12, listing his library 65

Lilium (Wood Lily) 69

Franklin's letter of March 20 with engraving of Union College 79

Mailing side of Franklin's letter of March 20 82

Syringa vulgaris (Common Lilac) 86

Lonicera hirsuta (Hairy Honeysuckle) 96

Dicentra eximia (Wild Bleeding-Heart) 114

Introduction

This book has been long in the making. In the fall of 1986, George Davis, our Hough Family expert at the museum, discovered these letters. We knew then that they would have to be published; their biographical value was immense.

The editor spent many months transcribing these manuscripts. Franklin's writing was difficult to decipher, but working on his diaries at the same time, one success spawned another. Now after many false starts, we have "come about."

It has been an agreeable task to work on Hough's writings. He was a voluminous author and correspondent. Unfortunately, the print-out of that period was by pen and ink. It took much longer, but did not seem to deter his productivity.

With the unfolding of this beautiful love story, there is great charm in the ingenious wording and spelling. It may have been the fashion in that day to use double consonants liberally, as in *untill*. They customarily used phonetic spellings such as *anaversary*. Punctuation was variable, more often left out. The reader is advised to accept these vagaries as customary for those times. The editor has purposely omitted footnotes that might disturb the flow of the letters.

Alongside these letters are occasional brief excerpts from Hough's diary, rounding out knowledge of those early months of 1849. Included are reproductions of manuscript letters from each writer including the *maze* letter that Franklin wrote as a challenge to Mariah.

In appreciation of Dr. Hough's love of botanizing, the illustrations identify those flowers mentioned in the letters which he hoped to have in his garden at Somerville. The *Rosa eglantine*, or Sweetbrier rose, of storied fame, was one of Hough's favorites, possibly because of its sweet-scented foliage. This rose has been used in decorative form throughout the book.

Our artist, Rhonda Ortlieb, a senior at Lowville Central School, has been funded under the Mark Mihalyi Memorial Mini-Grant Program, offered through the Lewis County Historical Society, for a work project devoted to Lewis County history. She has an impressive portfolio, but this is her first success as an illustrator of books.

There are no likenesses of either Franklin or Mariah at the time the letters were written. A daguerrotype of Franklin, mentioned in these letters, which he had made for Mariah, has never been found. Mariah was just a few days short of her 21st birthday and Franklin was 27 years old when they were married.

—*Vivian G. Smith,* Editor

Acknowledgements

Special thanks are due to George Davis, custodian of the Hough Family collection, now housed in the Hough Room at the Lewis County Historical Society Museum at the Gould Mansion. He located all twenty-three letters which had been scattered over the years.

Thanks to Edith Pilcher, biographer of Franklin B. Hough, for her several contributions to this book, prodding us to get into print and continuing enthusiastic support. Her appreciation of Hough ever multiplies.

Thanks to a fine Board of Directors of this Society who gave me the joy of a "go ahead." We commend Barbara Evans, Executive Director, and Jan Mooney, office secretary, for their choice of the manuscript type used in the letters, which adds grace and character to the contents.

Finally, our sincere appreciation goes to the late Patricia Hough, great-granddaughter of Franklin and Mariah, for the gift of Hough materials and a generous monetary legacy making possible adequate, safe, and attractive housing for these treasures.

Preface

When first reading the love letters of Franklin B. Hough and Mariah E. Kilham, I felt like an eavesdropper, since these were clearly meant for no one but each other. However, I quickly realized that their publication is a wonderful contribution to history; they provide a rare and intimate view of the private side of a great man's life. Such a romantic chapter enlivens and enlightens the conventional view of Hough as an austere, brilliant and extremely hard-working man.

Seldom has a courtship been conducted so fully by mail, or on such a high intellectual level. Only one visit relieved their separation, during the period of four months in which Franklin wooed and won his second wife. The delightful relationship which developed between them attests to the fine character and broad interests of its two principals. In the tradition of "arranged marriages," this one was "self-arranged," with remarkable delicacy and judgment.

He was a recently-widowed and newly-graduated country doctor, 27 years old, with a baby daughter being cared for by her maternal grandparents, while he struggled to conduct a widely-spread medical practice in Saint Lawrence County in northern New York. Apparently, he had committed himself to a year of mourning for his first wife, who had died in June, 1848. However, by the following January, his need for domestic companionship was so great, that he sought a new friendship which could develop into a lifelong love. It started with a tentative first step—writing to a former student who, he recalled, had possessed a "zeal for the acquisition of knowledge." They had first met some years previously, when he had taught at district schools in order to finance his way through college and medical school.

She was a young teacher in the country elementary school at Turin, on the eastern end of the Tug Hill Plateau, overlooking the Black River Valley. Flattered by his attention, she assured him of her esteem but felt the need to stress her inadequacies. She responded to his first letters shyly but sympathetically, displaying a congeniality of interests and feelings. Slowly she blossomed, under the depth of his interest in her and a vision of a shared lifetime of love and learning.

Just three weeks after the first letter, he visited her to propose marriage and was quickly accepted. Although only 60 miles apart, the severe winter weather, poor state of the roads, and demands of his practice kept them separated thereafter, until their wedding day on May 16th. As they kept their relationship hidden from almost all acquaintances until after their marriage, their letters reflected the added spice of secrecy.

Who else would court a lady, writing a tantalizing maze of a letter which would require hours to decipher? Who else would incorporate in a love letter a full listing of every book in his library, added to a description of "The Society for The Acquisition of Useful Knowledge"? It is fun to see his humor punctuate a recitation of work and scientific labors, as his careful formality gives way to a playful and ardent nature, and finally to expressions of renewal and rapture.

Their love lasted a lifetime, enriched by the birth of four sons and four daughters, all of whom were carefully nurtured. The family home in Lowville was pleasant and comfortable, reflecting their varied interests and capabilities. It incorporated at least four desks or tables, set aside for Franklin's exclusive use, as "recreation" for his restless nature lay in moving from one absorbing project to another. No wonder he wrote so many papers and books; his lifelong productivity was inspired by wellsprings of inner harmony and a loving wife.

—*Edith Pilcher*

Franklin B. Hough, c. 1860

Biography of Franklin B. Hough

by Edith Pilcher

He was a teacher, physician, geologist, botanist, meteorologist, archeologist, historian, statistician, civil servant, forester and ground-breaking conservationist. He expended as much time and energy on his avocational interests as on those that brought him an income, and his broad areas of scholarship were so diverse that he transcends easy classification. It is impossible to encapsulate the towering genius of Franklin B. Hough in a brief outline.

Franklin was born in Martinsburgh, New York in 1822, son of Horatio Gates Hough, the first physician to settle in the region. His father inspired in the boy early powers of observation and deduction, as well as interest in flora, fauna, stars, weather and every type of natural phenomenon. Franklin's boyhood collections of geological and botanical specimens were later expanded and attracted outstanding scientific recognition.

He started his education in a one-room school, and then went on to the Lowville Academy and later the Black River Institute in Watertown. This preparation enabled him to enter Union College in Schenectady in 1840 with advanced standing, and he graduated three years later, despite the fact that he had attended only spring and fall sessions, because he worked as a teacher in Champion and Turin during summers and winters to pay his college tuition.

His early interest in science led him to attend the Cleveland Medical College, and again he financed his education by teaching in country schools. Maria Eggleston of Champion became his wife during the summer of 1846, and in October 1847, gave birth to their daughter. She never recovered her health after the baby's birth, and died in June 1848 at Champion, shortly after his graduation from medical school. Franklin had just bought a medical practice and house in Somerville, near Gouverneur, in St. Lawrence County.

His mother kept house for him for several months while he started his work as a country doctor; it was during the latter part of his first year that he discretely wooed and then married a second wife, Mariah Ellen Kilham of Turin. While living in Somerville, he had ample time and opportunity to indulge his interest in minerology and botany; he exchanged correspondence and specimens with such leading scientists of that day as Louis Agassiz, Charles Shepard and Henry Boche. His rock collections were later sold to museums and universities.

During this period, he also collected fossils and other archeological specimens, and became interested in the early history of the surrounding region. These interests began to supercede medicine, and after four years, he gave up his practice to devote himself to historical research and writing.

While working in Albany on historical records, he managed to find various jobs in state agencies, which meagerly supported his growing family, and also did some editing for publisher Joel Munsell, who took an interest in his county histories. Finally, he secured a full-time position as Assistant to Joel Headly, then New York's Secretary of State, and was then appointed Superintendent of the State Census for 1855. This work marked his growth as a statistician; he was the first to include agricultural and industrial records in a census; this model was widely copied by authorities in other states and at the national level.

Hough also made major contributions to the State Gazette in 1860, and later to the 1873 edition. Piling one type of job on top of another, he worked on Indian treaties, legislation, treasury records, educational affairs for the Board of Regents, meteorological records, the first Civil List, and he gave frequent lectures at the Albany Institute. Papers and letters on a wide variety of topics issued from his pen in a never-ending stream; he kept abreast of scholarship in every field.

Between 1853 and 1860, Hough's histories of St. Lawrence, Franklin, Jefferson and Lewis Counties were published. These were the first in that region, and are still highly respected as definitive references. In 1861, he built a home in Lowville; he had grown temporarily weary of city life and cynical about state affairs. But, he plunged back into the thick of action when the Civil War began, becoming a Sanitary Inspector and then Surgeon for the 97th New York Regiment. His zeal for improving medical services then led to assignments in Washington, D.C., first in hospitals and then in the Bureau of Military Statistics.

After the war, Hough again became a civil servant, Superintendent of the New York State Census for 1865 and also heavily involved in preparations for the State Constitutional Convention in 1867. Next he supervised preparations for the Federal Census of 1870, and in the course of this work—collecting agricultural and trade statistics—became urgently aware of the decline in lumber production.

This led to his interest in reforestation, and to his drafting of the federal Forest Preserve Act, and the creation of a federal agency on forestry in the Department of Agriculture, which he headed until 1883, breaking new ground as one of the first conservationists. He wrote a classic treatise concerning the influence of forests on rainfall and climate, floods and droughts and attended international geographical meetings, at which he delivered his papers and reports. He also founded and edited the *Journal of American Forestry*.

He was working on research in Albany in 1885, when he became fatally ill. As usual, he had neglected his health, ignoring growing weakness and a lung inflammation. Pneumonia and heart complications set in, finally forcing him to bed. He died in Lowville shortly before his 63rd birthday.

Hough has received many honors and awards over the years. A new mineral which he had discovered was named Houghite in his honor. Union College awarded him an honorary A.M. degree shortly after his graduation. The State Board of Regents posthumously conferred a Ph.D. in Education in recognition of his history of that Board. An Adirondack peak in the Dix range, formerly known as Marshall, was renamed "Hough" in 1942.

His greatest renown today is as "The Father of American Forestry." His early conservation efforts were acclaimed by the American Association of the Geographical Congress in Venice; these and other writings were also acclaimed by a Prussian forestry expert, Bernhard Fernow.

Closer to home, he is credited with playing a major role in the creation of the New York State Forest Preserve. He shared honors with Verplank Colvin for the text of the First Annual Report of the Commissioners of State Parks, which emphasized the vital necessity of retaining the watershed forests to conserve water resources in the State and maintain canals. In 1935, during a 50th year celebration of the Forest Preserve, an historical marker was erected in front of his home which still remains. It reads: "The Forest Act of 1885 was enacted largely because of the vision and efforts of Franklin B. Hough, first New York forester."

A listing of Hough's published books and papers runs some 26 pages of small print! It does not include his unpublished works, many of which are equally significant. He ascribed this impressive productivity to the fact that he needed only four hours sleep per night, so he could accomplish much of his writing while others slept. Few scholars today, even utilizing all the wonders of copy machines and computers, could match his record of achievement.

The Kilham Family

Mariah Kilham was born in Turin, May 30, 1829, the daughter of Mariah and Heman Kilham. She was educated in the Turin schools. One of her teachers was Franklin B. Hough who taught in Turin for two terms in 1841 while enrolled at Union College for the spring and fall sessions. Franklin also opened a select school in Turin in the fall of 1847 before returning to Western Reserve at Cleveland, Ohio, to complete his studies in medicine. Mariah undoubtedly attended his classes during these years as she was one of his prize pupils. Following this, she taught school in Turin for two years.

Mariah's father, Heman Kilham, died in October 1848, at an early age. Her grandfather, Thomas Kilham, emigrated by ox cart from the Westfield, Connecticut area in 1799 with many others, seeking new opportunities in the wilderness of northern New York. According to Hough's *History of Lewis County**, Thomas died in 1825 from an opiate given in overdose by a drunken physician.

Mariah's mother, also Mariah, was born in Canaan, Massachusetts. She had been a resident of Turin since she was 24 years old and died there at age 92. Her second husband was a Mr. Crofoot.

Widowed for twenty-five years, Mariah Kilham Hough died in 1910 at the Hough family home on Collins Street in Lowville, as the result of complications from a fall down stairs. Four sons and one daughter survived of their eight children.

* Hough, Franklin B., *History of Lewis County*. (Albany: Munsell & Rowland, 1860) p. 211

The Letters

Somerville, St. Lawrence Co, Jan. 15, 1849

Respected Friend,

It may perhaps excite surprise to receive a communication from me, since although we have been personally known for several years yet that acquaintance has never assumed the form of a written correspondence. I remember with pleasure the interest you took in the study of botany, and still earlier in by-gone years the zeal with which you engaged in the elementary studies of the District School; when we had to each other the relation of Teacher and Scholar. Presuming that this zeal for the acquisition of knowledge has continued till the present, I have ventured to write and solicit the pleasure of your correspondence, not doubting but that I may derive much advantage and pleasure from your further acquaintance.

Should the above proposal meet with your concurrence, you will do me a great favor by writing soon, directing to me at this place.

With much esteem I remain,

Yours ____,

Franklin B. Hough, A.M.M.D.

Jan. 22/49

Mr. Hough Sir

Yours of the 18th I received and perused bygone years. How vividly do those halcyon days of happiness rise in my memory, the days spent with my young friends in childish sport and innocent amusements. Yes, remember well the first time I went through Arithmetick it was at your school.

Grammar—Likewise there was a great interest taken in, you probably remember about it (especially the prize).

Those days are past and gone but others present themselves (other school days) yes I am now in the capacity both of scholar and Teacher. I have charge of 4 classes, the 1st & 2nd Arithmetick, a reading class and the 1st & 2nd Grammar. You know that is one of my favorite studies especially Krisklaus.

I take but two studies they are History and Latin. I am about half way through the grammar in the conjugation of verbs. How Long do you think it will take me to finish the study of Latin? It is rather dry yet difficult to remember though I Look for the better, and hope it will not be in vain.

If my writings will compensate you for yours (as I am afraid they will not) I shall be very happy to receive another letter before long as I can proffit thereby; for I am a scholar yet when writing to you a Teacher.

This from your friend

Mariah E. Kilham

P.S. You will be kind enough to let me know how long you think it will take to finish Latin (in your next letter)

Please write soon if agreeable

F. B. Hough: A.M.M.D.

Somerville, Jan 26, 1849

Dear Friend, Your kind letter of the 22nd inst. was received on Monday. I have been prevented by interruptions and incessant calls upon my time for answering sooner. The physician has a hard life to live, as he is not master of his own time, but liable to be called away in all weather, and at any hour in the twenty four. My business has been prosperous since my residence here although much of the time has been very healthy. In ordinary years my charges (good bad and indifferent) will not be less than $800 or perhaps $1000 per annum. This year (9 months) although several times away several days at a time, I have charged more than $600. So you see that the profession though laborious is rather profitable. At least much more so than that of a teacher. I look forward to the time when my debt for the pleasant home I purchased will be paid in the course of three or four years. But perhaps you may care but little about my business and I will say no more. I had forgot that I was writing to a lady correspondent, and that the subject of our letters was to have been something intellectual - - - something profitable to the mind.

I am favorably situated for collecting minerals ____ being in the midst of numerous localities and I have accumulated large quantities for exchange. My collections previous to 1849, I sold to the Cleveland Medical College. They numbered about 1000 specimens and they are now in the museum of that institute. I have exchanged quite extensively since but have not prepared cases for arranging them and they are packed in boxes. Did you ever pay any attention to this study? There are few of your sex that can devote much attention to mineralogy unless they have access to cabinets. Some of the most discriminating mineralogists I have known were ladies. Perhaps you may think minerals rather hard food for the mind but one who has a thirst for learning can digest everything and out of it elaborate useful knowledge. If I mistake not you are one of these and would if you had the opportunity take the greatest pleasure in any department of Natural history, if favored with books, and instruction from those competent to teach. How few there are who possess the first qualification for teaching the Sciences! What little I have ever been so lucky as to acquire, although but little, has been by my own exertions with the aid of good books. Botany, Mineralogy, Geology and the sister sciences are taught in our academies by those who are ignorant of the principles and have an aversion to the pursuit of these studies. You may think me censorious upon a subject where my opinion is gratuitous but such is my opinion on these subjects.

You ask my opinion about the length of time it takes to acquire knowledge of Latin. A lifetime would be too little to read and admire all the Latin writers. The Classics usually read viz Virgil, Sallust,

Cicero, Caesar, Horace, Juvenal and Nepos, require from two to three years, daily study. This gives one an ability to read fluently, write and speak passably, and translate elegantly, any Latin author. It also opens an avenue to the Italian, Spanish, French and Portugese languages which can all be quickly learned by a good Latin scholar. But the greatest benefit to be derived from the study of the Latin is the knowledge it gives one of his native tongue, the force of language can be fully understood only by one who knows the signification of the component parts of which it is made up. You have entered upon a wide field. Have you counted upon the time and labor incident to the undertaking? But what are your plans of life! What use do you propose to make of these acquirements? Perhaps you propose to spend your life in teaching. If so you have selected an arduous and responsible duty. In forthcoming numbers of the Northern Journal you will see a series of articles with my initials as a signature, on the teacher's calling. You will often meet with communications in the "Journal" and the "Democrat" from me; sometimes with, at other times without a signature or with some fictitious name attached. Did you read the articles in the Democrat a year or more since, signed "Viator"?

But possibly this correspondence in which you are engaged may change your plans of life, if they are not immutable. You are aware of my condition in life, - - of my circumstances and you must be familiar with the old saying that men under these circumstances are by turns melancholy, inquiet, restless and unhappy.

If I have committed an indiscretion in the course of this letter I hope to be forgiven. Perhaps by it I may loose a much valued correspondent. Perhaps I have offended a sense of delicacy or excited surprise, that so early in a correspondence or at all an allusion has been made to a theme of momentous importance which but few persons who attain mature age do not discuss inwardly and in the silent recesses of the heart, if not otherwise.

Should you not think proper to answer this letter you are requested to commit it to the flames and bury in oblivion former recollection of the writer. It will give me sincere pleasure however on the other hand to receive a communication from you in reply at as early a day as you may find convenient.

With the greatest esteem

I remain,

Your Friend.

Franklin B. Hough

Claytonia Virginica
{Spring-Beauty}

Turin Feb 4th/49

Dear Friend

Your interesting letter of the 26th inst. I obtained on Thursday. I was much pleased to hear of your success in business though regret that it is so fatiguing both to body and mind, but I trust and hope you will be amply rewarded for your unwearied pains in preparing for so responsible and arduous a station.

It has given me pleasure for years to hear of your prosperity in all your undertakings. You wrote me you were favorably situated for collecting minerals and had accumulated large quantities for exchange. I think it must be very pleasant to be so situated. I very much regret that I have thus far neglected the study of Mineralogy, Geology and the Sister sciences but be assured it has not been for want of an inclination to pursue them but for want of a good opportunity; though I have ever anticipated the period when I shall not be wholy ignorant of these interesting branches.

You asked me if I had thought of the time it requires to get a knowledge of Latin I was well aware it would take a long time. My object was to get a better knowledge of my native tongue though I was anxious to read and translate readily.

You wished to know my plans for life. I have been unable to execute the plans I have so long contemplated, for want of means. As for teaching I never intended to teach but one term more then spend a year or two at school that I might be better fitted for efficient action in the world.

It discourages me to hear <u>*you*</u> *speak of the little you have acquired. What think you of my acquirements which are but a drop compared to the ocean. Can I bury in oblivion the recollections of* <u>*one*</u> *to whom I am so much indebted for useful instruction, not only when we were in the capacity of Teacher and Scholar but since then! No my feelings are to the reverse of that, and will stay until memory bids me a final farewell and I no longer find pleasure in the endearing bonds of friendship. Shall I cease to appreciate the many favors granted to one who is already trespassing upon your time.*

The piece you have reference to (signed Viator) I have not seen though I have heard it spoken of, it was supposed to be written by F. B. Hough but am waiting patiently for the coming Journal which contains your writings upon the "Teachers Calling".

I wonder if this pleasant moonlight evening is one of your lonely ones? I hope not. You may be affording relief to the sick whilst I am regretting that you are even found as a victim of lonliness for I have too long been one to sympathize with thee, "dear friend". I have well known what lonliness is since the death of a kind Father and a beloved sister, but such is life.

This from your sincere friend

Mariah E. Kilham

P. S. I have beat Mary as I have finished my letter and she is still writing casting now and then a rougish glance this way to see what I write, perhaps I better not tell who she is writing to though I will if you would like to know.

How do you like living in Sommerville? Have a pleasant society I presume.

May I be favored with another of your kind epistles before long (when convenient for you).

Turin Feb 4th /49

Dear Friend

Your interesting letter of the 26th inst. I obtained on Thursday. I was much pleased to hear of your success in business though regret that it is so fatiguing both to body and mind, but I trust and hope you will be amply rewarded for your unwearied pains in preparing for so responsible and arduous a station.

It has given me pleasure for years to hear of your prosperity in all your undertakings. You wrote me you were favorably situated for collecting minerals and had accumulated large quantities for exchange. I think it must be very pleasant to be so situated. I very much regret that I have thus far neglected the study of mineralogy Geology and the Sister sciences but be assured it has not been for want of an inclination to pursue them but for want of a good opportunity; though I have ever anticipated the period when I shall not be wholy ignorant of these interesting branches.

You asked me if I had thought of the time it requires to get a knowledge of latin I was well aware that it would take a long time. ~~though~~ my object was to get a better knowledge of my native tongue though I was anxious to read and translate readily.

You wished to know my plans for life. I have been unable to execute the plans I have so long contemplated, for want of means. As for teaching I <u>never</u> intended to teach but one term more. then spend a year or two at school that I might be better fitted for efficient action in the world.

It discourages me to hear <u>you</u> speak of the little <u>you</u> have acquired. What think you of my acquirements which are but a drop compared to the ocean. Can I bury in oblivion the recollections of <u>one</u> to whom I am so much indebted for useful instruction, not only when we were in the capacity of Teacher and Scholar but since then! No my feelings are to the reverse of that, and will say until memory bids me a final farewell and I no longer find pleasure in the endearing bonds of friendship Shall I cease to appreciate the many favors granted to one who is already trespassing upon your time.

The piece you have reference to (signed viator) I have not seen though I have heard it spoken of, it was supposed to be written by F B Hough but am ~~coming~~ waiting patiently for the coming journals which contain your writings upon the "Teachers Calling"

I wonder if this pleasant moonlight evening is one of your lonely ones? I hope not. You may be affording relief to the sick whilst I am regretting that you are ever found as a victim of loneliness for I have too long been one not to sympathize with thee (dear friend). I have well known what loneliness is since the death of a kind Father and beloved sister. but such is life.

this from your sincere friend

Mariah E. Tiller

P.S. I have beat Mary as I have finished my letter and she is still writing casting now and then a roguish glance this way to see what I write, perhaps I better not tell who she is writing too (though I will if you would like to know)

How do you like living in Hammond? have a pleasant society I presume

May I be favored with another of your kind epistles before long (when convenient for you)

Paeonia
{Peony}

Somerville, Feb. 9, 1849

Dear Friend, *Your second epistle was received yesterday and read with real satisfaction. From the tenor of your letter I am led to infer that you are disposed to cultivate my acquaintance to any extent consistent with honor, and I am happy in believing that in you I have found a true and sympathizing friend, with whom I can confer on terms of more strict intimacy than with the generality of the class which in the language of the world are denominated friends. How little does that expression mean, as it is usually applied. Some hold it as synonimous with relative, or acquaintance, but how wide is often the difference! A relative has been justly(?) defined, as one who can rob one if rich, or insult him if poor. If this is true they do not come under the class of true friends. There is something peculiary pleasant in having one to whom can be confided the secrets of the heart, to whom every care, every hope and every sentiment can be freely imparted, and who sympathizes with ones successes and sorrows at his misfortunes as if they were its own, —who resents an injury or defends the cause of the other in his absence and who is truely and in every sense of the word a friend. There exists in society a relation in which this community of feeling and mutual friendship may be cultivated to perfection and become a source of the purest happiness which mortals are permitted to enjoy. This is the Domestic Circle. What enjoyments cluster around the fireside, and how much may the friendship and mutual assistance, consolation and advice of the domestic relation tend to soften the asperities, and render pleasant the journey of life. Have you thought of this? Had such a train of thought entered your head when writing or reading our letters? Having known the pleasure of the unreserved confidence and true friendship arising from this source, you will not wonder that I have felt desolate and friendless, since nearly a year ago the hand of death rudely snatched from my side a friend of the class I have above alluded to.*

If I am not much mistaken you possess a sympathizing heart and are capable of a warm and abiding friendship of the true kind; and from expressions in your letter I flatter myself that I am not altogether an object of indifference to you. I cannot doubt but that these expressions of regard represent the true feelings of the heart, and that as a confidential friend you would be as enduring and as worthy of friendship as it could be possible. If I am an impartial judge of my own heart these sentiments are reciprocal. Perhaps few persons have as small number of confidential associates as myself, yet those few will testify that no one is more warm in his friendship, or more true in his attachments. During my academic and collegiate course I scarcely contracted a single friendship which I was desirous of perpetuating by a correspondence. I used every one with civility and kindness and was respected in turn, but yet they were not of a kindred spirit. While some sought pleasure in walking the streets and visiting places of amusement, or poured over some classical author, or found in the social circle his happiness, I retired to the fields and groves or along the margin of some lake or river where I could study the works of nature in all their loveliness.

The only college acquaintance which I maintain by correspondence or which I would give three cents for keeping was a companion of many a rural ramble and like myself an enthusiastic admirer of the Natural Sciences. He is a Mr. Arnold of Fairfield. Through his influence I procured the appointment of principal in the Fairfield Academy one of the finest institutions in the state. I was compelled to decline from having a few days previously bound myself by purchasing in Somerville. Perhaps some who have known me might call me cold hearted because they found me disposed to keep my business my thoughts and feelings to myself yet everyone must be allowed his own way in making choice of confidents. It is a privilege which they cannot deprive one of. I shall be under the necessity of visiting Lewis County on business before long and shall endeavor to see you. I may propose question of momentous importance and I shall be very happy to receive an answer in the affirmative. You must from the tenor of this letter infer what it will be. From the nature of my profession and the fickle change of weather as well as the state of the roads I am not able to appoint a day but I think it will be either Wednesday, Thursday or Friday of next week (Feb 14, 15, or 16th) that you will see drive up to your mother's house a cutter with somebody in it sometime between sundown and dark. Should I fail to appear you will I hope ascribe it to some necessity and not to negligence. I trust our correspondence is kept by you a profound secret.

I shall hardly have time to receive another letter from you before seeing you and shall therefore not expect one.

This evening I lecture at the Gouverneur Seminary—the second lecture of a course on Geology and the Sister Sciences. They are attended by crowded houses and my audience is very intelligent and respectable. It is a cold inclement day and I dread the journey (6 miles) but it is not half so bad as to turn out into the storm of midnight, and face the sleet and freezing rain eight or ten miles as I have done more than once. I get nothing for lecturing but the self satisfaction of imparting truth and the growing reputation of a man of "erudition and science".

From your true and sincere friend

Franklin B. Hough

GOUVERNEUR N.Y.
10
FEB

PAID 5

Maria C. Kilham.
Turin.
Lewis County
New York

III.

Feb. 9. 1849.

From the diary of Franklin B. Hough. March 25, 1848 - Jan. 13, 1852.*

Feb. 14, 1849 Started precisely at mid-night in cutter for Martinsburgh and Turin. Went by way of Carthage. Arrived there about 6 ocl. Staid 2 hrs. and then went on through Denmark, Lowville and to C. Arthur's. Exchanged my horse for one of Iva Sheldon's and went on to Martinsburgh village where I procured the first volume of Paleontology. Went to Bingham's and got my contributions to S.A.U.R. Returned. Went to H. Hough's. W.D. Yale's and to Mrs. Kilham's where I spent the night.

There was contracted an agreement which will last for life with Maria(h) E. Kilham, a former scholar and ever a favorite friend of myself. How solemn and aweful when seriously considered is this momentous question! And how much does it need of candor and sound discretions in making choice of a companion for life!

If I am a candid and impartial judge this match will be agreeable and every way calculated to confer happiness upon both parties.

It is the understanding that this marriage shall be consumated early next summer if not before. No time was set but the day and other arrangements relating will be left to the parties of the "second part".

By a coincidence which had not been premeditated this bargain was concluded on Valentine's Day and the Valentine present was of course the hand and heart.

* The early diaries of Franklin B. Hough are in the possession of the Lewis County Historical Society Museum, Lyons Falls, New York.

Hepatica Americana
{Round - Lobed Hepatica}

Somerville, Feb 19, 1849

Dearest Maria, Having learned that the office of Town Superintendent is biennial and not to be filled till next year I have concluded not to defer writing till after the town meeting. I reached Copenhagen the first day and Somerville the second after leaving your house. As the roads were much drifted I did not visit my child as they live 8 miles from the direct road. At the Great Bend I stopped and procured a daguerreotype portrait which my friends have pronounced the most striking and perfect likeness they ever saw. I procured it to send to you my dearest Maria, when your brother calls upon me on his journey into the country.

I wish you to keep it as long as you live and when I am absent you can turn to it and read the features of your true and affectionate friend and future husband as they were the day after we pledged to each other our hearts and hands. Perhaps on our marriage day we may get another taken in which we shall stand as in the hour when we were pronouced man and wife.

I will also lend you my scrap book which contains all I ever wrote for the papers, and send Elisha C. a copy of my perpetual or "rotary calendar". I trust James will not fail to call upon me when he comes this way as I would not fail to send these articles.

A transaction has lately occurred at Governeur which has made a most forcible and salutary impression upon me. Three days ago a young woman swallowed half an ounce of cedar oil for a criminal purpose and died in a few minutes. Two weeks previous her paramour came to me secretly in the night for medicine or medical assistance. I indignantly rejected his magnificant reward and urged upon him an honorable marriage. He will be sent to the States Prison and I shall be a principal witness against him. Had I yielded to his importunities I might have been now his companion, tenant of the criminal cell in Canton jail. Thus have I been fortified in Moral Courage, and shall better be able on another occasion should one occur, to say no. Even if he had procured the oil of me my career in Somerville would have been at an end, and the people would have sought out and established another more worthy physician. I hear as I am around the village the remarks like these which were not spoken for my ear. "That was doing right," "He is a man of principle," "If we have such a Doctor among us we cannot prize him too highly" scsc. I know dearest Maria that you will share my pleasure in thus having escaped a snare into which others might have fallen, and know too that your sympathies and influence will always be with me to keep me from erring from the path of honor and virtue.

Tuesday, Feb 20

Dearest Maria. I had proceeded thus far with my letter yesterday when a sheriff entered my home with a mandate to appear forthwith at Governeur on the examination of the wretched and misguided Noah Fleming. Today I am subpoened to appear before the grand jury in Canton. Tomorrow he will be tried and probably sentenced to States Prison for life! A neighboring physician will but narrowly escape with the loss of his reputation, while on every side I hear nothing but praise and commendation and not the least that I withstood the offers of an express messinger sent by the prisoner a few minutes before the sheriff, to induce me to refuse to testify, which if I had done the public would have believed to have been from conscious guilt. No offers or inducements have prevented me from appearing and testifying to the whole truth. I cannot express my dear Maria, the pleasure arising from an approving conscience, and am happy in knowing that there is a heart which vibrates in unison with my own, that sympathizes with every joy that feels every sorrow, and that in every walk of life will be my trusty and confidential friend, to whom every wish and thought of the inmost soul may be disclosed and who in joy and in sorrow, in the sunny days of prosperity or the storm of adversity will cling to my interests and share in my emotion with more true interest than a brother. That relation in life is more endearing than any other mankind is permitted to enjoy. Shall we not prove living example of that unchanging constancy—that undying love, for which as the scriptures say—one will leave home and friends and every endearing association of early years? 'Tis a solemn thing to leave the home of early childhood—the paternal dwelling and society of brothers, sisters and parents, to bid adiew to every fond association and early companion and pledge before heaven to spend a lifetime with all its possible changes and vicissitudes with another!

Yet what enduring relations arise from the change. A common interest a common drive and a common home.

Home! What associations cluster around the word. And although you may bid a parting adieu to the spot you have hitherto called home with a tear, yet I hope and trust that you will find in the home of your Franklin a home you would not exchange at any future period. To sit down for the first time at the table which you have spread,—to preside at the fireside which will in all the coming time of life be yours, will be a sensation of pleasure which will make a lasting impression upon your mind.

If constant kindness, undying affection, and unceasing care to alleviating the cares of a beloved wife can accomplish it your lids shall never be sullied by a tear, your breast never heave with a sigh, or a penitential regret steal for a moment over you that you have forsaken your pleasant family circle for the residence of another, —that you have pledged your heart on the altar of love and vowed eternal friendship and alliance at the shrine of Matrimony.

Accept these hastily written lines as a token of affection and confidence with the assurance that you are never absent from my thoughts,—that you are a theme of pleasing day dreams and a beloved object of affection and esteem.

By your affectionate friend,

Franklin

Could my letters be directed to James with the mark FBH in the corner so that you could get them?

Feb 25, 49

Dear Franklin

At length have I found a moment which I may improve in sweet converse with thee how delightful the employ thus to commune with a spirit pure and bright as thine; methinks such friends (as thou art) are as the oasis in the desert, or as a bright spot in the dreary void of existence. Indeed! what would life be divested of the pleasing intercourse of kindred hearts?

My dearest Franklin little can you imagine the pleasure imparted by the perusal of your excellent letters. It is truly an "intellectual feast" proceeding only from a mind conversant with the beauties of nature, and taught to expatiate upon the follies of the World.

There is but one fault I find with your epistles that is they are so short. I believe if you should write four times as much they would be too short. Dear Franklin (for I may with good heart call you so) if I could write as you can I would take a larger sheet than this and fill every side.

I cannot be thankful enough that my Dear Franklin escaped the snare which has entangled a brother physician I can well say (with your neighbors) "it was doing right". You are a man of principle. Since I saw you time has flown swiftly and joyously by life being fraught with much to make it pleasant and desireable as you well know that the society of friends and the acquisition of knowledge are among the most elevating enjoyments of which the human mind is susceptable. Indeed I wish that these bright days may always last. I have wished that the joyousness of school days might never be over but alas a change has come . . . and what it envisions for the future to unfold yes I have bid adieu to the long loved school room do you think it was with regret that I have done so? No, at view of the prospective rendered my last school days pleasant rather than dreary, though it was rather solemn to think that I never should be in the capacity of scholar again surrounded with the many dear associates that were with me that day and wondering why I left before the close of the next term my excuse was I had so much work that must be done before teaching in the summer therefore I could not attend any longer so it passed off with no further inquiry.

Perhaps you would like to hear a word about our exhibition. It passed off very pleasantly with the exception of the noise. There was a very large congregation assembled to view the performance many more than could get into the church. At the close of the exhibit the schollars took an oyster supper at Woolworths which was rather pleasant, though would have been pleasanter if you had been one of the group.

Whilst at the table Lavantia said Mariah did Uncle Franklin call at your house the other day? Yes said I; but what could I have said or done if she had quized any farther. I presume she thought nothing of it as I have for years been accustomed to inquire after you; but I have been rather shy for a few weeks. I'll assure you and I trust I shall not always be in such a predicament that I shall be afraid to speak of one so confiding as thou art.

The cold formalities and passing civilities of fashionable friends I lightly esteem but a true friend I prize above any thing else on such I can rely entire confidence. The "Miniature" of such a friend will be happily received and I shall be half inclined to think I am conversing with Franklin if I receive your scrap book in connection with it. I am fearful I shall not receive them as James may not call on you if he does not what shall I do. You will please send them the first opportunity will you? I wish it was here this delightful twilight hour that I might gaze upon the features of a true friend excuse these hastily written lines and accept them from your unworthy yet devoted

Mariah

You can direct your letters to James first as well as not we shall know the writing.

Somerville, March 1, 1849

Dearest Mariah,

Your very acceptable letter with a beautiful card and still more beautiful sentiment was gratefully received. I use in writing this sheet that bears the seal of a Society in Union College to which I belonged. The hands are a token of friendship; the E.U. means "Equitable Union" the name of the society and the Greek initials O.A. (ouden adelon) signify "Nothing Concealed", for true friendship withholds no secret from the heart to which it confides. Yet how shallow the depth of friendship among members of such a society when compared to the pure deep and gushing fountains of love which spring from the hearts of those who are bound by the silken chain, of those who have pledged before Heaven a mutual regard, constancy, an attachment which nothing but the ruthless hand of death severs and which through every vicissitude of life shall remain to sustain and encourage in adversity, or to congratulate in prosperity.

You spoke of Lavantia's inquiries. You need not deceive yourself. She and her mother doubtless mistrust the whole affair. I have not been out for nothing, having no visible necessity to call me and yet not able to go two miles further and visit them? Mother is about to go home soon. Most likely within the week. I will send those articles in a sealed package to Walter D. Yale who will deliver them at your house. He will probably open the package. He knows the whole story but I know him too well to doubt his ability to keep a secret! But what will become of me??? Almost every hour in the day some one is calling on some business or other. How long shall they knock at the door of an uninhabited house? With whom can they leave their messages? Who will prepare me a warm cup of tea or coffee at an unreasonable hour at my return home from a long and fatiguing ride? Who will with ready needle repair the loss of a button or give timely attention to some slight tear in my coat? Who will sympathize with every joy and every sorrow? These are questions for you to answer. Do not Dearest Mariah, infer from these inquiries that I want a wife for the sole purpose of receiving the messages of my patrons, of mending or taking care of my clothing,—far from it. Hirelings would do that as well as any one. My necessities are of a different nature and if I can judge of my own feelings of a purer and more ennobling kind, not the least is a desire to hear the end of the importunities, gossip, false stories and provoking offers of advice and assistance in procuring a partner for life with which I am daily beseiged in my daily rounds.

My journey to Turin gave additional cause for surmises.

I will tell you a circumstance which is itself sufficiently ludicrous. I have been for years acquainted with the family of Abram Baslow in

Philadelphia, Jefferson Co. Some weeks ago I called in passing to borrow some cloth to wind around a house plant I was taking home. He has two daughters, one with a foul blemish on her character, the other red headed, tall and far from being of the right sort. Very soon after Mr. B. was passing through Somerville and took occasion to inquire all about my business prospects and character. On my return from Turin I called again to leave the cloth and being urged hard stopped to take supper. A day or two after one of his sons was passing through this place called at the post office and made all the inquiries you could imagine about me and gave his reasons, that I was paying attention to his sister!!!! She has been out in this neighborhood for several days as I am told, but I have not seen her, nor dont wish to. I certainly never gave the slightest occasion for her to take the trouble. It is ridiculous to see what fools some will make of themselves. If Mr. B. ever thought that I had the slightest idea to taking his daughter he is surely mistaken. She may have wealth and education but they are trifles when bestowed upon a red head, freckle face long and lean form of a family of blemished character. Although irritated and harassed by such idle tattle now I shall be still more when I come to be left with the house to myself alone. I shall take my meals at a neighbor's but my time will be spent when at leisure in my lonely house. You will I hope take pity on my lonliness and hasten the time when our hands shall be united as are now our hearts in the holy bonds of Matrimony.

How think you will it seem to you to be called Mrs. Hough? It will seem strange at first doubtless but you will become soon accustomed to it. I inclose a map of my house constructed in accurate proportions also the first two articles printed two years ago in the N. Jour. My articles on Education it seems have miscarried or have been lost, sent to a private person and he may have lost or forgotten them. This and its mate which I will send in my next you may give to Mary as I have it in my scrap book. I forgot entirely when out to see you that custom requires that permission be obtained of the parent when a member is to be taken from a family. Perhaps the ceremony may yet be gone through with when I —

Now, dearest Mariah you will take pity on my lonely condition wont you? I hope you will not ascribe my anxiety to a selfish or improper motive, as I hope that I am as free from such as yourself. Nothing but the purest friendship the most ardant attachment has led to this engagement and nothing shall ever occur on my part to render the tenor of our future life but pleasant and delightful. If you will write a large sheet of paper one thickly with your thoughts next time it will be read with the greatest pleasure by your affectionate

Franklin

Having reached the end of my letter before arriving at the end of my subject I am induced to give it a second time going over with like one gets in company with an absent friend he is very apt to set up late to talk so when an opportunity offers to hold sweet converse with his absent though very dear friend the temptation may be too strong to be resisted. Perhaps before you have deciphered the whole of this letter sleep may steal as irrestibily upon your eyelids as when at your house after being deprived of my usual repose for several days and nights. Do you remember the first sweet kiss we ever exchanged? Do you remember the second kiss? Do you not look forward with a pleasing anticipation to the thousandth?

It has been observed that this visable manifest token gets after a little while to be an old story. This may not be so in our case for there is something to me of a very tender and endearing nature in the warm hearted affectionate and lingering pressure of the lips upon the object I love.

My little girl is the only person I have been free to bestow this token of affection, the kiss, and sometimes she would fight and struggle against it, yet as she grows older she will first feel of my face and if it is smoothly shaven will press her innocent little lips upon my cheek in a manner so loving that it does one's soul good to see—much more to feel it. If I am a judge of the character of a child she will make a most affectionate and kind-hearted daughter and should the time come when she would become a member of our family would doubtless make a most cheerful amiable and dutiful girl. Yet how many disasters seen and unseen hang around the path of a child—and how numerous and how narrow the escape which they meet with before they arrive at maturity. The path of life from the cradle to the grave is thickly strewn with thorns and cares and happy must be the one who escapes untouched by them.

Have you dearest Mariah counted on the crosses and the unpleasant perplexities that assail the house keeper and which assail the most favored of those that travel the journey of life. You doubtless have cast a prospective glance over the field before you have like myself resolved that whatever unpleasant or disagreeable that may rise in the course of the future life shall be met with in the temper and spirit of a philosopher and adopting the sentiment and spirit of the poet Pope exclaim "Whatever is is right."

Whatever fault you may see in me I hope you will always have the kindness to point out to me in a spirit of tenderness and kindness and by mutual concession a charitable construction upon every action which though apparently wrong though arising from a motive and by mutual and unreserved confidence we may be able to esteem each other more highly from day to day and from year to year.

That such may be the result of our union and such the tenor of our lives is the ardent wish of your

Franklin

P.S. Please to inform me whether you have taken the pains of decyphering the whole of this letter or most. If you have I consider it as unerring token of sincere regard and shall be confirmed of the belief that I am not entirely an object of disregard by yourself.

Somerville March 1. 1849.

Dearest Maria

Your very acceptable letter with a beautiful card and still more beautiful sentiment was just received. I use for writing this a sheet that bears the seal of a society in Union College to which I belonged. The hands joined are a token of friendship; the E. U. means "Equitable Union" the name of the society and the Greek initials, O. A, (ouden adelon) signify "Nothing concealed," for true friendship withholds no secret from the heart to which it confides. Yet how shallow the depth of friendship among members of such a society when compared with the pure deep and gushing fountains of love which spring from the hearts of those who are bound by the silken chain, or of those who have pledged before Heaven a mutual regard and constancy, an attachment which nothing but the relentless hand of death can sever, and which through every vicissitude of life shall remain to sustain and encourage in adversity, or to congratulate in prosperity.

You spoke of Lavantia's [?] inquiries. You need not deceive yourself, she and her mother doubtless may [?] know the whole affair. "I have not been out for nothing, having no visible necessity to call me and yet not able to go two miles further and visit them." Mother is about to go home soon. Most likely within a week. I will send those articles in a sealed package to Walter Tyack [?] who will deliver them at your home. He will probably open the package. He knows the whole story but I know him too well to doubt his ability to keep a secret.

But what will become of me ...?? Almost every hour in the day some one is calling on some business or other.

How long shall they knock at the door of an uninhabited house? With whom can they leave their messages? Who will prepare me a warm cup of tea or coffee at an unseasonable hour at my return home from a long and fatiguing ride? Who will with ready needle repair the loss of a button or give timely attention to some slight tear in my coat? Who will sympathize with every joy and every sorrow? These are questions for you to answer.

to end of [illegible]

[illegible]

Do not deem it [illegible] from these inquiries that I want [a] wife for the sole purpose of receiving the messages of my patrons or of mending or taking care of my clothing — far from it. Hirelings would do that as well as any one. My necessities are of a different nature and if I can judge of my own feelings of a purer and more ennobling kind. Not the least is a desire to hear the end of the impertinence, gossip, false stories and provoking offers of advice and assistance in procuring a partner for life with which I am daily beseiged in my daily rounds. My journey to Irvin gave additional cause for surmises. I want to tell you a circumstance which is in itself sufficiently ludicrous. I have been for years acquainted with the family of Hiram Baslior in Philadelphia [illegible]. Some weeks ago I called in passing to leave some cloth to [illegible] around a house plant which I was taking home. He has two daughters one with a foul blemish on her character, the other red headed, tall and far from being of the right sort. Very soon after Mr B was passing through Somerville and took occasion to enquire all about my business prospects and character. On my return from Irvin I called again to leave the cloth and being urged have stopped to take supper. A day or two after one of his sons was passing through this place called at the post office and made all the enquiries you could imagine about me and gave as his reasons, that I was paying attentions to his sister!!! She has been out in the neighborhood for several days as I am told, but I have not seen her nor don't wish to. I certainly never gave the slightest occasion for her to take the trouble. It is ridiculous to see what fools some will make of themselves. If she is [illegible] taught that I had the slightest idea of taking her daughter he is sadly mistaken. She may have wealth and education but they are trashy when bestowed upon a red head, freckled face long and lean form, and family of blemished character.

Although annoyed and harrassed by such idle tattle now I shall be still more when I come to be left with the house to myself alone. I shall take my meals at a neighbor's but my time will be spent when at leisure in my lonely house. You will I hope take pity on my loneliness, and hasten the time when our hands shall be united as are now our hearts in the holy bond of Matrimony.

How strange will it seem to you to be called Mrs Haugh. It will seem strange at first doubtless but you will become soon accustomed to it.

I inclose a map of my house constructed in accurate proportions — also the first of two articles printed two years since in the N. Jour. The articles on Education it seems have miscarried or have been lost. I sent them by a private person and he may have lost or forgotten them. This and its mate which I will send in my next you may give to Mary as I have it in my scrap book. I forgot entirely when out to see you that custom requires that permission be obtained of the parent when a member is to be taken from a family. Perhaps the ceremony may not be gone through with when I —

Now dearest Maria you will take pity on my lonely condition won't you. I hope you will not ascribe my anxiety to a selfish or improper motive, as I hope that I am as free from such as yourself. Nothing but the purest friendship the most ardent attachment has led to this engagement and nothing shall ever occur on my part to render the tenor of our future life [illegible] pleasant and delightful. If you will write a large sheet of paper over thickly with your thoughts next time it will be read with the greatest pleasure by your affectionate Franklin

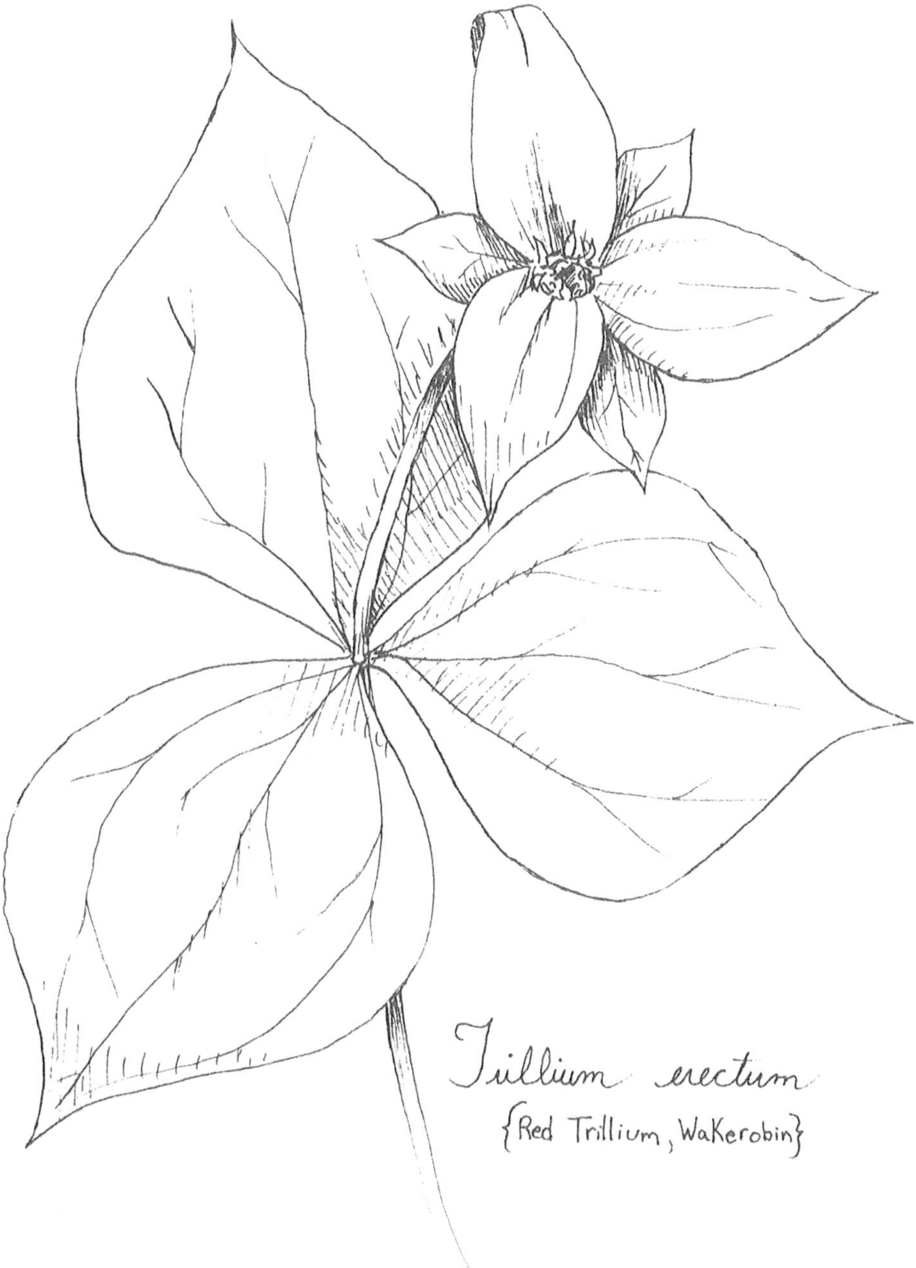

Trillium erectum
{Red Trillium, WaKerobin}

March 4, 1849

My dear Franklin

With pleasure I acknowledge the reception of your kind letter which I called to the office for yesterday and obtained. I asked if there was anything for me then and in answer received one for James with FBH signed to it. Do you not think that I know who it was from as soon as I saw it? Indeed I did.

Dearest Franklin I am very sorry your Mother is going to leave you so soon. Can you not induce her to stay any longer. I think you must be very lonely, but if you get a good boarding place it will not be as bad as though you were home all of the time but "Whatever is, is right" and we must make the best of it. You may wish whilst alone as I am now writing for a true warm hearted friend who can sympathize with you in all of your feelings, in which you can trust at all times and to whom you can open your whole heart and not fear her answer.

And before many months your wish may be realized the exact no. I cannot tell yet. Whilst we are debarred of each others society we prize highly (or I do at least) written communications. I hope you do not think my memory so treacherous as to forget the warm embrace of one I love so dearly. No I shall never forget until my eyes are closed in death and I have had a final farewell to all I love on earth (and then perhaps not). I should be discouraged at once if I believed the observation "that this visable manifest token of affection and love gets to be an old story after a while."

No it will not be so in our case if I can hinder it. If I thought our attachment would be weakened (instead of strengthened) I never would think of being married. An inward throbbing tells me very different from this.

My dearest Franklin I feel as though I could remain through every vicissitude of life to sustain thee in adversity or to congratulate thee in prosperity and trust that you do the same.

How vast the difference in the friendship of two of the same society and that of two who are engaged to each other companions for life.

I shall look for that package every day until it arrives. I hope I shall not look in vain for the miniature of my dear Franklin. Oh! how it appears that you are in pretty good demand among the Ladies you may tell them they can't all have you, their hearts will be broken will they not?, especially the Misses Baslow do you not pity them? I do.

I visited your sister, Mrs. Woolworth, yesterday afternoon had a very pleasant visit indeed your name was not mentioned to me but your sister came to Mary before we left and said if Franklin comes out again tell him that he has a sister living not far off. I was perfectly surprised to hear that she said it though am not since reading your letter. I hope she will keep it in the dark.

I have been very busy since I left school to work at everything we have quilted two quilts and have another on the frame it is best to get the large work done first.

I have just seated myself by the window to enjoy the beauties of the evening. The moon sheds her silvery light upon the earth and the few changing clouds give enchantment to the scene! All is still and serene each chord of my heart stirs and vibrates responsive to nature's music. I imagine I hear the whispering of the departed in every breeze. Perhaps dearest Franklin is seated and indulging in the dreamy reveries of the mind if so I wish him pleasant thoughts.

As for your letter I decyphered every word and with a good deal of pleasure too. You must take good care of yourself when you are alone and think you will not be alone always. I ought to say something in reference to my new neighbors though I will wait until I see them and get acquainted all I care for then is that they take good care of you. From your true and affectionate

Mariah

You will please excuse this letter as it is my thoughts penned down as you wished this sluggish pen will poorly communicate to you what I could tell if I were with you.

March 4th 1847

My dear Franklin

With pleasure I acknowledge the reception of your kind letter which I called to the Office for yesterday and obtained. I asked if there was any thing for me there and in answer received one for Jane, with F B H signed to it. Do you not think that I knew who it was from as soon as I saw it? Indeed I did.

Dearest Franklin I am very sorry your Mother is going to leave you so soon. Can you not induce her to stay any longer. I think you must be very lonely but if you get a good boarding place it will not be as bad as though you were at home all of the time but "Whatever is is right" and we must make the best of it. You may wish whilst alone as I am now, only for a true warm hearted friend who can sympathize with you in all your feelings in whom you can trust at all times and to whom you can open your whole heart and not fear her censure.

And before many months your wish may be realized. the exact time I cannot tell yet. Whilst we are deprived of each others society we prize highly (I do at least) written communication.

I hope you don't think my memory so treacherous as to forget the warm embrace of one I love so dearly. No I shall never forget until my eyes are closed in death until I have bid a final farewell to all I love on earth (and then perhaps not) I should be discouraged at once if I believed the observation "That this visible manifest token of affection & love gets to be an old story after a while."

No it will not be so in our case if I can hinder it. If I thought our attachment would be weakened (instead of strengthened) I never would think of being married. An inward throbbing tells me very different from this.

My dearest Franklin I feel as though I could remain through every vicissitude of life to sustain thee in adversity or to congratulate thee in prosperity and trust that you do the same.

How vast the difference in the friendship of two of the same society and that of two who are engaged as each others Companions for Life

I shall look for that package every day until it arrives hope I shall not look in vain for the Miniature of my dear Franklin. Oh! ha! it appears that you are in pretty good demand amongst the Ladies you may tell them they can't all have you their hearts will be broken will they not? especially the Misses Barlow do you not pity them? I do.

I visited your sister Mrs Woolworth yesterday

afternoon had a very pleasant visit indeed your name was not mentioned to me but your sister came to Mary before we left and said if Franklin comes out again tell him that he has a sister living not far off I was perfectly surprised to hear that she said it though am not since reading your letter. I hope she will keep it in the dark.

I have been very busy since I left school to work at every thing we have quilted two quilts and have another on the frame it is best to get the large work done first.

I have just seated myself by the window to enjoy the beauties of the evening. The moon sheds her silvery light upon the earth and the few ranging clouds give enchantment to the scene (All is still and seems each chord of my heart stirs and vibrates response to nature's music. I imagine I hear the whisperings of the departed in every breeze. Perhaps dearest Frank is seated and indulging in the dreamy reveries of the mind if so I wish him pleasant thoughts.

As for your letter I decyphered every word and with a great deal of pleasure too. You must take good care of yourself when you are alone and think you will not be alone always. I ought to say something in reference to my new neighbors though I will wait untill I see them and get acquainted all I care for them is that they take good care of you. from your true and affectionate Mariah

You will please excuse this letter as I my thoughts penned down as you wished it This sluggish pen will poorly commence to you what I would tell I know with you

Somerville, March 12, 1849

Dearest Mariah,

Your letter of last week was received in due time but necessary business has rendered it inconvenient to reply till now. You see upon this sheet the emblem of a Lewis County society, "The Society for the Acquisition of Useful Knowledge"—founded April 18th 1843, dissolved by mutual consent Sept 12, 1848. This emblem is of my own drawing and invention, and the engraving is in my possession. The All Seeing eye indicates that a benificent Deity is always watching over us, and wherever we may wander, in fields or forests,—among the habitations of mankind or in the rural solitude we are the special objects of Providential care. The triangles have reference to a Mathematical problem of great interest, and they, with the eye, are used by the Jews in their synagogues, as an emblem of Divinity—embroidered in gold upon satin, and suspended before the shrine which contains the Sacred Law.

The triangles and circle denote the precision and symmetry which every where pervades creation while the rays denote the splendor of the beauties with which a kind Providence has everywhere adorned the earth.

The society died for want of sufficient interest being felt by the generality of its members in its meetings. Its collections went to their donors. Yet it served to call together a few kindred spirits who will cherish each others friendship till long after the society shall have been forgotten. Yet how different this friendship from that which unites two willing hearts of opposite sexes but congenial spirits and who see in each other those qualities of taste and mental endowments which give assurance of prolonged and constantly increasing happiness!

The package with miniature that I sent on Tuesday by a man who will place it in the hands of Walter Yale by whom it will be left with you. Preserve the scrapbook with great care as I would not loose it for worlds. Its loss could not be repaired. Give the calendar to Mary's beau and the loose number of "correspondence" to Sister Mary. I trust you have recieved these long ago safely.

Mother left on Tuesday last and I am alone most of my time in my lonely house when I am not on my errands of mercy to the Sick. You dont know how lonely it is to come home to my house and set down to build a fire and spend the evening without a human being in the house. No one will rent the house unless assured of possession for a year which is out of the question you know. The neighbors have set upon me like a pack of frantic wolves and I cannot appear in a store, or tavern, without being assailed on the subject of marriage. I trust you will commiserate my destitute condition and abbreviate the time which shall elapse before we are united as man and wife. I would not urge with improper importunity, but cannot conceal my wish for the time to arrive when I can sit by my own domestic fire-side—and possess a home to which I can invite a friend—or extend the rites of hospitality to a stranger:—at which I shall meet as I return home an affectionate and warm hearted wife—the partner of life's joys and sorrows, the confiding friend, and participator of the lights and shadows of earthly existence. I esteem among the greatest of the pleasures of life to receive and reciprocate the friendly calls of relatives and neighbors. One cannot be practiced with credit without the other also and I am consequently for the present cut off from intercourse with the world. A widower is always regarded as an object of superstitious dread by some, avoidance by others and of public notice and remarks by all.

What young lady would have the audacity to enter my house to have a tooth extracted? or to exchange a library book?—or even to send for me to go to her own house in case of indisposition for fear of public gossip. He is public property and everybody seems under a necessity to make his own remarks or to promulgate the gossip of others. Wherever he goes he is watched, his friendship is attributed to some sinister motive, and the eyes of the whole community are intent upon him. To be freed from this unpleasant position is one of the minor motives which have actuated me in this engagement. I rely upon your affectionate regard, the sincerity of which I cannot for a moment doubt, to free me from my dilemma at as early a day as may be consistent with suitable arrangements. Meanwhile, you may rest assured that you are never long absent from my mind—and that the anticipation of the happiness which a voice within promises will yet be mine, in your society, will contribute to make me cheerful and patient during the time which although is seems comparatively short, yet will seem an age, ere the Silken Chain of destiny shall unite us in a union, which death alone shall sever. How pleasing yet how solemn the thought and reckless must be that character that could hastily and in levity form this alliance without first pausing to take a survey of the prospect before him. I trust that there will be no occasion for either party to regret for a moment the engagement, or repine at the result of an acquaintance which has I trust for years been a source of pleasant recollection, and which for long years to come will have a source of unfading and heartfelt happiness.

Yet the nearest and tenderest relations of life are sundered by death! The fairest rose will wither,—and the wasting sickness or sudden dispensation will tear from our embrace the cherished objects of our affection, and desolate the fairest and fondest prospects of the heart.

The gloomy certainty of death is to me a theme of frequent reflection yet I endeavor not to mourn over the necessity which will one day put a period to my own existence.

It is very sickly about here just now and this letter is written in moments hastily snatched from intervals between professional calls.

Not long since I made out a catalogue of our library, presuming that you will examine it with some interest I will copy it into this letter.

†*	Nat Hist of New York - Vols	18
†	Taconic System	1
†	Tables of organic Remains	1
†	Brande's Encyclopedia	1
†	Medical Volumes	18
†	Olmstead's astronomy	1
	Barrits " & atlas	1
	Ferguson's "	1
	Spofford's "	1
†	Silliman's Journals (bound)	6
†	Dana's Mineralogy	1
†	Philips "	1
	Comstock's "	1
	Emmon's "	1
†*	Manual of Classical literature	1
	Kane's Chemistry	1
	Grays "	1
	Comstock's "	1
	Liebeg's "	1
†	Macquer's "	2
†	Blairs lectures "	1
	Blairs (small) "	2

	Pamphlets	9 vols
†	Almanacs	15
	M.S.S. Notes	15
	Greenleaf's gram	1
	Kirkhaus "	1
	Smith's "	1
	Bullions "	1
	" (small) "	1
	Alexander's "	1
	Taylor's "	1
	Ueboter's "	1
	Murrys "	1
	" exercises "	1
	Eatons Geological Manuel	1
	Mather's Geology	1
	Comstocks "	1
†	Ohio State "	1
	Vermont "	1
	New York " (annual)	5
	Marsh's Book Keeping	1
	Bennetts "	1
†*	Gourand's Muemonics	1
	Carmina Sacra	1

	Bible (4 to and com size)	2
†	*Patent office reports*	2
†	*Lindley's nat sys Botany*	1
†	*Eaton & Wrights*	1
	Mrs. Lincoln	2
†	*Flora Astrica*	1
	Muhlenberg's grammica	1
†	*Curier's animal kingdom*	4
†	*Hist Berks & Lebanon Co.*	1
†	" *York & Lancaster Co.*	1
	" *U. State Hales*	1
	" *Universal*	1
	" *Seige of Londondery*	1
	" *Ohio*	1
†	*Davies surveying*	1
†*	*Wilson's ornithology*	1
*	*Handbook of oil painting*	1
*	*Combe on Constitution*	1
*	*Science & art of industry*	1
*	*Hitchcock's Gold manual*	1
*	*Student's manual*	1
*	*Reliqueal Baldwinianene*	1
	Smith's epitome	1
*	*Guycots Hist civiliz*	1
*	*Wayland's moral sci*	1
*	*Abbot's Teacher*	1
*	*Taylor's dist school*	1
	Halls lecture of school Keeping	1
	Jour. Franklin Institute	2
*	*Lardners Lectures*	1
	Brewster's optics	1
	Trego's Geog Penna	1
*	*Paleys theology*	1
	Laws of etiquette	1
*	*Pamphlets and tracts*	1
	Village Reader	1
	Rhetorical "	1
	Angels (5th)	1
	Emmersons (1st)	1
	Academical "	1
	Introduc Eng. "	1
	Amer Preceptor	1
	U.S. Speaker	1
	N.A. Reader	1
	French Grammar	1
	Nugent's Dictionary	2
	spelling Book	1
	Class Book	1
	Testament Italian	1
	Grammar (Vassai)	1
	dictionary	1
	Guide to Rome Latin	2
	And & Stoddards Gramm	1
	" " *Reader*	1
	" *Exercises*	1
	" " *Key*	1
	Eton Grammar	1
	Jacob's Reader	1
*	*Authors Cicero*	1
	" *Sallust*	1
	Latin tutor	1
	Virgil	1
	Davidsons Virgil	1
	Cicero de oratore	1
	Cicero de officius	1
	Cordevious	1
	Westminster lessons	1
	First "	2
	Dictionary	1
	Horace	1
	Livy	1

Greek	
Lessons	*1*
Grammar	*1*
Exercises	*1*
Testament	*1*
Iliad	*1*
Lexicon	*1*
† *Covaeca Majora*	*1*
Perkins Arithmetic	*1*
† *Pikes* "	*1*
Dabol's "	*1*
Tracy's "	*1*
Ruger's "	*1*
Bennetts "	*1*
Adams "	*1*
Smiths "	*1*
" *new* "	*1*
* *Day's Mathematics*	*1*
" *Algebra*	*1*
Honnycottes "	*1*
† *Forsyth on Forest titles*	*1*
Olmsted's Philosophy	*1*
Juvenile Philosophers	*1*
Schenectady directory	*1*
Thayer's Geography	*1*
Willets "	*1*
Huntingtons "	*1*
Woodbridges "	*1*
Goldsmiths "	*1*
Ladies Companion	*1*
Young's night thoughts	*1*
Starks European guide	*2*
Butters compendium	*1*
Whateleys logic	*1*
Humboldts Travels	*1*
Sea Voyages	*1*
Spectator 8th vol	*1*
Phonograph reader	*1*
" *class book*	*1*
Ossious Poems	*2*
Burns "	*2*
Beatties Poems	*1*
Popes essay on Man	*1*
Science of Government	*1*
Asamen on Aurora Bound	*1*
Ohio gazetteer	*1*
" *citizens guide*	*1*
Medical electricity	*1*
Missionary Herald	*1*
Scrap books	*3*
Dist sch journals	*1*
other volumes (small)	*40*

These make about 197 volumes besides stacks of pamphlets and unbound numbers of journals ____. Our district library kept at the office contains 100 volumes, so that you will have an abundance of food for the mind. Perhaps you may think me at too much trouble in writing a "love letter" all over with a catalog of books. The interest you are presumed to take in my affairs henceforth may perhaps justify the *measure. This mark (†) I have prefixed to books of a large size and (*) those which are elagantly bound. I have about 20 volumes herbarium,—about 200 indian antiquities (stone)—50 or more coins (copper) and about 4000 or more specimens of minerals and fossils & shells besides duplicates for exchanging.—I anticipate much pleasure in looking over these extensive collections with you and in the assistance I shall derive from your aid and sympathy in prosecuting my studies and inquiries.*

I had hoped to be able to visit Martinsburgh and of course Turin about the first of April but must try to get my business done by letters. It is so sickly around here now that I could not leave at any rate short of absolute necessity. There is a loss attending my absence from my business besides loosing the calls that may come during the time I am away—People will get the habit of sending elsewhere if I am not to be found usually when sent for. I have slept but one whole night for a week. I trust you will have the goodness and regard for my loneliness not to defer the occasion of a visit on "Necessary business" to your house longer than the month of May. Would it not be a harbinger of future happiness if our hands and hearts were united in the lovely dawning of Spring—the month of flowers? Now you will set some period not distant for this ceremony won't you? My home is so lonesome and I am so much an object of charity that I hope you will regard my situation with compassion.

I have a chance (I learned lately) to receive a family (a young man and his wife—the tailor of the village)—into my house and board with them. He is building a house which will be ready in August. It will be unpleasant to have two families in the house for a part of the summer. It of course will not be expected by you that our union could be delayed till then. I could not think of it. I will await your answer before I make any bargain with him. I shall rent the house conditionally—that half of it be relinquished when demanded, —or shall I keep the house empty a few weeks longer? You know how unpleasant it would be to have two families at a time in the house. Consult your own wishes and your pleasure will be mine. Write soon so that I can receive the letter Friday if possible. Meanwhile as I approach the end of my letter I must wind up by urging you not to postpone the subject I have pressed upon your determination. Consider my destitution, my necessities and my anxieties. How lonely it is to spend the long evenings in solitude. How empty and heartless the attentions received from hirelings—summer friends—who serve one's wants for the hope of money.

From your ever affectionate and true lover and bosom friend

Franklin

Somerville March 12. 1849,

Dearest Maria!

your letter of last week was recieved in due time but
necessary business has rendered it inconvenient to
reply till now. You see upon this sheet the emblem
of a Lewis County society, "The Society for the acquisition
of Useful Knowledge" — founded Apr 1843. dissolved
by mutual Consent Sept 2. 1848. This emblem is of
my own drawing and invention, and the engraving is in my possession.
The All Seeing Eye, indicates that a beneficent Deity is always watching
over us, and wherever we may wander, in fields or forest, — among
the habitations of mankind, or in the rural solitude we are the special
objects of Providential care. The triangles have referance to a Mathematical
problem of great interest, and they, with the eye, are used by the Jews in
their Synagogues, as an emblem of Divinity — embroidered in gold upon
satin, and suspended before the Shrine which contains the Sacred law,
The triangles and Circle denote the precision and symmetry which
every where pervades creation, while the rays denote the splendor of the
beauties with which a kind Providence has every where adorned the earth.
This society died for want of sufficient interest being felt by the generality
of its members in its meetings. Its collections revert to their donors. Yet it served
to call together a few kindred spirits who will cherish each others friendship
till long after the society shall have been forgotten. Yet how different this
friendship from that which unites two willing hearts of opposite sexes but congenial
spirits and who see in each other those qualities of taste and mental endowments
which give assurance of prolonged and constantly increasing happiness!
The package with miniatures &c I sent on Tuesday by a man who will place it in
the hands of Walter Gale by whom it will be left with you. Preserve the scrap
book with great care as I would not loose it for worlds. Its loss could
not be repaired. Give the Calendar to Mary's beau, and the loose numbers
of "Correspondence" to Sister Mary. I trust you have recieved these long ago safely.
Mother left on Tuesday last and I am alone most of my time in my lonely house
when out on my errands of mercy to the sick. You don't know how lonely it is to come
home to my house and set down to build a fire and spend the evening without a
human being in the house. No one will rent the house unless assured of possession
for a year & it is out of the question you know. The neighbors have set upon me
like a pack of prairie wolves and I cannot appear in a store, or tavern, without
being assailed on the subject of marriage. I trust you will commiserate my
destitute condition and abbreviate the time which shall elapse before we are
united as man and wife. I would not urge with improper importunity, but I
cannot conceal my wish for the time to arrive when I can sit by my own domestic
fireside — and possess a home to which I can invite a friend — or extend the rites of
hospitality to a stranger; — at which I shall meet as I return home an
affectionate and warm hearted wife — the partner of life's joys and sorrows, the
confiding friend, and participator of the lights and shadows of earthly existence

I esteem it among the greatest of the pleasures of life to receive and reciprocate the friendly calls of relatives and neighbors. One cannot be practised with credit without the other also and I am consequently for the present cut off from intercourse with the world. A widower is always regarded as an object of superstitious dread by some, avoidance by others, and of public notice and remark by all.

What young lady would have the audacity to enter my house to have a tooth extracted? or to exchange a library book? — or even to send for me to go to her own house in case of indisposition for fear of public gossip.

He is public property and every body seems under a necessity to make his own remarks or to promulgate the gossip of others. Wherever he goes he is watched; his friendship is attributed to some sinister motive, and the eyes of the whole community are intent upon him. To be freed from this unpleasant position is one among the minor motives which have actuated me in this engagement.

I rely upon your affectionate regard, the sincerity of which I cannot for a moment doubt, to free me from my dilemma at as early a day as may be consistent with suitable arrangements. Meanwhile you may rest assured that you are never long absent from my mind — and that the anticipation of the happiness which a voice within promises will yet be mine in your society, will contribute to make me cheerful and patient during the time which although it may be comparatively short, yet will seem an age, ere the silken chain of destiny shall unite us in a union which death alone shall sever. How pleasing yet how solemn the thought and reckless must be that character that could hastily and in levity form this alliance without first pausing to take a survey of the prospect before him. I trust that there will be no occasion for either party to regret for a moment the engagement, or repine at the result of an acquaintance which has I trust for years been a source of pleasant recollection, and which for long years to come will prove a source of unfading and heart felt happiness.

Yet the nearest and tenderest relations of life are sundered by death! The fairest rose will wither, — and the wasting sickness or sudden dispensation will tear from our embraces the cherished objects of our affection, and desolate the fairest and fondest prospects of the heart.

The gloomy certainty of death is to me a theme of frequent reflection yet I endeavor not to mourn over the necessity which will one day put a period to my own existence.

It is very sickly about here just now and this letter is written in moments hastily snatched from ^interruption^ professional calls.

Not long since I made out a catalogue of ~~my~~ our library. Presuming that you will examine it with some interest I will copy it into this letter.

†× Nat Hist New York —	vols 18.	† Dana's Mineralogy	1.	Pamphlets —	9 vols
† Taconic System —	1.	† Philips " —	1.	† Almanacs —	15
† Tables of organic Remains —	1.	Comstock's — " —	1.	M.S.S. notes,	15.
† Brande's Encyclopedia —	1.	Emmon's " —	1.	Greenleaf's Gram	1
† Medical Volumes —	18.	†× Manuel of Classical Literature	1.	Kirkham "	1
† Olmsted's astronomy —	1.	†× Kane's Chemistry	1.	Smith "	1
Burritt's " & Atlas —	1.	Gray's Comstock's " †	1.	Bullions "	1
Ferguson's — " —	1.	Liebig's — "	1.	" small Alexander's "	1
Spofford's — " —	1.	† Macquer's "	2.	Taylor's "	1
		† Blair's Lectures	1.	Webster's "	1
		" " (small)	2.	Murray's "	1
† Silliman's Journals (bound)	vols 6.	†× Espy's Philos of Storms	1.	" exercises "	1

Eatons Geological Manual — 1.
Mathers Geology — 1.
Comstocks " 1.
+ Ohio State " 1.
Vermont " " 1.
New York " " (annual) 5.
Marsh's Book keeping 1.
Bennetts " 1.
+* Gouraud's mnemonics — 1.
Carmina Sacra — 1.
Bible (4to and com size) 2.
+ Patent office reports 2.
+ Lindley's Nat Sys Botany 1.
+ Eaton & Wrights " 1.
Mrs Lincoln " 2 copies
+ Flora Cestrica (") 1.
Muhlenberg's grammar (") 1.
+ Cuvier's animal Kingdom 4.
+ Hist Berks & Lebanon Co 1.
+ — " York & Lancaster " 1.
" U States Hist [illegible] 1.
" Universal ([illegible]) 1.
" Siege of Londonderry 1.
" Ohio 1.
+ Davies surveying — 1.
+* Wilson's Ornithology 1.
+* Handbook of Oil painting 1.
+ Combe on Constitution 1.
+ Science & arts of industry 1.
+ Hitchcock's Geol manual 1.
+ Students Manual — 1.
+ Reliquiae Baldwinianae 1.
Smith's epitome — 1
+ Guyzots hist civiliz 1.
+ Waylands moral sci 1.
+ Abbott Teacher 1.
+ Taylors dist school 1.
Halls lectures on school keeping 1.
Four Franklin Institute 2.
+ Lardners Lectures 1.
Brewster's optics — 1.
Frego's Geog [illegible] — 1.
+ Paley's theology — 1.
Laws of etiquette 1
(Pamphlets & tracts 1.

Village Reader 1.
Rhetorical " 1.
Angells (5th) " 1.
Emmersons (1st) " 1.
Academical " 1.
Introduc Eng " 1.
Amer Receptor 1.
U.S. Speaker 1.
N.A. Reader 1.
(French)
Le Brun Grammar Telemaque 1
Nugents Dictionary 2.
Spelling book 1.
Class Book 1.
Testament 1.
Italian
Grammar (Bassi) 1.
dictionary 1.
Guide to Rome 2.
Latin.
And & Stoddards Gram 1.
" " Reader 1.
" Exercises 1.
" " Key 1.
Eton Grammar 1.
Jacobs Reader 1.
+ Anthons Cicero 1.
" Sallust 1.
Latin Tutor 1
Virgil 1
Davidsons Virgil 1.
Cicero de natura 1.
" " Officiis 1.
Corderius — 1.
Westminster Lessons 1.
first " 2
Dictionary — 1.
Horace 1.
Livy 1.
Greek
Lessons 1
Grammar 1
Exercises 1
Testament 1
Iliad 1
Lexicon

+ Graeca Majora 1.
Perkins Arithmetic 1.
+ Pikes " 1.
Dabolls " 1.
Tracys " 1.
Rugers " 1.
Bennetts " 1.
Adam's " 1.
Smiths " 1.
" new " 1.
Day's Mathematics 1.
" Algebra — 1.
Bonnycastles " 1.
+ Forsyth on Forest trees 1.
Olmsteds Philosophy 1.
Juvenile Philosophers 1.
Schenectady directory 1.
Mayes Geography 1.
Willets " 1.
Huntingtons " 1.
Woodbridges " 1.
Goldsmiths " 1
Ladie's Companion 1.
Young's Night thoughts 1.
Stark's European guide 2.
Butlers Compendium 1
Whatley's logic 1.
Humbolts Travels 1.
Sea voyages 1.
Spectator 8th vol 1.
Phonographic Reader 1
" Class book 1.
Ossian's Poems 2
Burns " 2
Beatties " 1
Popes Essay on Man 1.
Science of Government 1.
Warren on Aurora Borealis 1.
Ohio gazetteer 1
" Citizens guide 1
medical electricity 1
Missionary Herald 1
Scrap books 3
newspapers bound vols 3
Dist sch Journals 1
Other volumes (small) 40.

These make about 177 volumes beside stacks of pamphlets and unbound
numbers of journals &c. Our district library kept at the office
contains 108 volumes, so that you will have abundance of food
for the mind. Perhaps you may think me at too much trouble
in writing a "love letter" all over with a catalogue of books,
the interest you are presumed to take in my affairs generally
may perhaps justify the measure. This mark (†) I have
prefixed to books of a large size, and (+) to those which are
elegantly bound. I have 20 volumes herbarium, — about 200
indian antiquities (stone) — 500 or more coins (copper) and about
1000 or more specimens of minerals and fossils & shells, beside duplicates
for exchanging. — I anticipate much pleasure in looking over these
extensive collections with you and in the assistance I shall derive from
your aid and sympathy in prosecuting my studies and inquiries.
I had hoped to be able to visit Martinsburgh and of course Turin
about the first of April but must try to get my business done by
letters. It is so sickly around here now that I could not leave at
any rate short of absolute necessity. There is a loss attending
absence from my business beside, losing the calls that may come
during the time I am away. — People will get in the habit of sending
elsewhere if I am not to be found usually when sent for. I have slept
but one whole night for a week. I trust you will have the goodness and
regard for my loneliness not to defer the occasion of a visit on [illegible]
business to your house longer than the month of — May. Would it
not be a harbinger of future happiness if our hands and hearts [illegible]
united in the lovely dawning of Spring — the month of [illegible]
Now you will set some period not distant for this ceremony
won't you? My home is so lonesome and I am so much [illegible]
of charity that I hope you will regard my situation with [illegible]
I have a chance (I learned lately) to recieve a family (a young man
and his wife — the tailor of the village) — into my house and board with
them. He is building a house which will be ready for use in August.
It will be unpleasant to have two families in the house for a part of the
summer. It of course will not be expected by you that our union could be
delayed till then. I could not think of it. I will await your answer before I
make any bargin with him. Shall I rent the house conditionally — that half of it
be relinquished when demanded? — or shall I keep the house empty a few
weeks longer? You know how unpleasant it would be to have two families at a time
in the house. Consult your own wishes and your pleasure will be mine. Write soon
so that I can recieve the letter Friday if possible. Meanwhile as I approach the
end of my letter I must wind up by urging you not to postpone the subject
I have here pressed upon your determination. Consider my destitution
my necessities and my anxieties. How lonely it is to spend the
long evenings in solitude. How empty and heartless the attentions we recieve
from hirelings — summer friends — who serve one's wants for the hope of money!
From your ever affectionate and true lover and bosom friend
Franklin

IV

March 14. 1849.

Lilium
{Wood Lily}

Turin, March 15th, 1849

With a great deal of pleasure I seat myself, pen in hand to converse with my dearest Franklin for a while. Your long looked for letter arrived yesterday, it was received and perused. with not a little interest I'll assure you.

I wonder if it affords you the pleasure to peruse my letters that yours do me.

You can not imagine the pleasure it affords me to seclude myself in some retired spot with a bundle of letters to read again and again; they bring to mind many pleasing recollections of acts which transpired in by-gone years and were it not for these tokens of friendship would ever be thought of again, but - - - dear Franklin the few letters I have received from thee afford me much more enjoyment than any letter connected with the above bundle.

My dear Franklin how greateful we ought to be that we can cultivate that "attachment" that exists between us, (if not by seeing each other) by the frequent interchange of our own ideas however <u>wayward</u> and <u>eccentric</u> mine may be, think not if I do fail to interest that it is for want of a disposition to do so; but ability.

That package was delivered here yesterday in my absence. The first thought that suggested itself upon looking at it "oh that those lips had language". It seems almost as though you were here when I look at it. It is a striking likeness and one that I prize above all others.

Your request in regard to my saving the scrapbook was not made in vain. I find it very interesting though have read but little yet as time will not allow.

Mary is very much pleased with her pieces and says she is very grateful that she has a so kind a brother in a pleasant village where it is always summer (ville). - - - She anticipates a great deal of pleasure in spending a few weeks with us there in persuing those branches (Botany & Mineralogy) that we so much admire; for we hold the enjoyment of Nature's scenes to be among the choicest of earth's pleasures; though the great maw shut their eyes to such gifts, and beauties, passing through life as if their whole cup of bliss was to live and breathe insensible, inanimate and dead; still we are content to indulge in the happiness such contemplations afford.

And why not? Why should the innumerable portions of Earth which are not necessary to the support of man's animal existence, have been strewn so thickly around us had they not been designed for our benefit and enjoyment?

When shall our hands like these are pledged be joined? I have concluded some pleasant evening in May—please decide in your next letter upon the day of the month and your decision shall be mine if I can get ready as I very much regret that you are placed in so lonely a condition and the thoughts too of your being constantly exposed to the gossip of the world.

I want you should act your own plan (and it will be mine) in reference to letting your house though I should think it would be pleasanter for you to let them in if they are fine people, pleasanter than to take your meals away, then return to a cold house, and be all alone, it will be a very short time for two families to be in one house until August though do just as you choose it will soon pass away. If you rent the house, which part shall you reserve or shall you rent the whole?

I think you or we must have a very nice library and should take great pleasure in looking it over and I shall derive a great benefit thereby. I am very sorry to hear that you are so disturbed of your rest, be careful and take care of your own health.

I should be very happy to see you in April as you spoke of though it will be demanding too much of you though I shall see you as I have you here.

I have chosen white muslin for my bridal dress, how do you like it; white is an emblem of purity you know, some have an aversion to the white, if you have I would like to know it. Please write as soon as convenient that I may not send to the Office so many times in vain and accept this from your affectionate

Mariah E. Kilham

Somerville March 20, 1849

Dearest Mariah

Your letter of the 15th was received yesterday. I hasten to reply to it and have selected a sheet of paper which tho' it has been singed by an unlucky accident yet bears a representation of objects connected with many a pleasant association of bygone years—the seat of literature and science—to which memory will sometimes wind back and linger around the scenes of other days and call up the scarsely remembered features of classmates and teachers.

Yet the halls that resounded with the eloquence of declamation, the earnestness of debate and the more quiet recitation, and the chapel that echoed the solemn voice of prayer—are forever closed to me. The distant scenery was the haunt of many a silent hour and as from the summit of the highest hills in the background I was wont to survey the stinted pine oak forests interspersed with green fields—secluded hamlets and wandering streams I would often indulge myself in a pleasing revery and as I meditated on the site of the ancient Council fires of the Iroquois confederacy the half consumed coal and brands of which still blacken the hill tops around the city I could not forbear experiencing a sensation of sadness at the change that equally awaits individuals as well as nations—and which in some coming time may equally befall our own happy land—and the institution which I have learned to call by the endearing name of Alma Mater. It is but justice to remark in relation to this picture that the terrace in front; the two buildings in the foreground and the colonades extending back from them are the only portions of Union College yet built. The chapel in the centre and the back buildings are yet to be erected.

My room was in the left hand (north) college at the window marked with a dotted line and the letter A.

I have been boarding for the last week in the family A C Van Dyke my nearest neighbor at 12/ per week washing and mending included. I lodge at home and seldom stay in my boarding place except at meal time. I have not had much time at home lately as it has been and is now quite sickly.

Sometimes I build a fire in my office and sit down to study my Medical works or to read your letters over.

None of my patients have died lately although several have been so sick—children especially that their lives were despaired of. They are all convalescing.

No one but a physician can tell the heartfelt pleasure which is felt as at each succeeding visit the sufferer is found a little better. I believe parents themselves cannot feel more pleased. I have seen within the last week many evidences which leave me to infer that I have secured and am increasing in the confidence of my employers, the anxious yet confiding appeal of the heart stricken parent cannot fail to excite the sympathies and call forth the energies of the attending physician and I am frequently placed in a situation where my responsibilities bear heavily on my shoulders and nothing but a confidence of ability and skill in the use of remedies could sustain me in the prosecution of my calling.

I derive daily more confidence in my own abilities and in the efficacy of my remedies, and look to the time, dearest Mariah when I shall enjoy a reputation in my profession which shall extend beyond the precincts of my own town and vicinity and envision a competence for an old age, and for a day when I shall support myself and family by daily industry. At the age of thirty if life and health are spared to you and me I shall be free from debt and the owner of my home—with outstanding accounts besides, on interest, to the amount of several hundred dollars. In relation to our bridal dress, I am without any preferrence or choice. Female dress is scarcely even an object of notice or observation by me.

I am perhaps too little particular about my own dress but must depend upon the taste and attentions of a wife for a suitable appearance. I even strive to escape particular notice by having the fashion of my clothing no way remarkable either for newness or oldness of its style. By following the medium I hope to pass without attracting observation or remarks.

Respecting "The Day" I would propose Wednesday May sixteenth, at 8 ocl. A.M. so that we might reach home the same evening.

I have ever looked upon ostentation and parade at weddings as the height of folly particularly the long train of carriages which for miles will attract the attention of the inhabitants by exciting the remark—"Wonder who is married now?" Much pleasanter in my opinion would it be to ride off in a private carriage alone, attracting no attention and eliciting no remark. If I should express a wish in relation to the wedding it would be that the party invited should consist only of Relatives and the most intimate friends. I am not strenuous in these matters. If you have other preferences it will be my pleasure to favor them. I shall not rent my house to the man as I spoke of. Meanwhile I will whitewash and paint it within (and without perhaps) so that you can begin housekeeping without any previous trouble in cleaning. I will provide provision of all kinds to be all ready by the time above referred to.

Would you have the knot tied by Mr. Hurd? We want some one to do it strong. Meanwhile be assured that I remain as ever

Your affectionate Franklin

March 20

Any different arrangements than those within which you may suggest will be adopted at once by me. The remarks apply only to myself and contain my own views in relation to what I consider pleasant and suitable for such an occasion.

FBH

A

Union College.

Somerville March 20. 1849

Dearest Mariah

Your letter of the 15-th was recieved yesterday. I
hasten to reply to it and have selected a sheet of paper
which tho' it has been singed by an unlucky accident
yet bears a representation of objects connected with many
a pleasant association of bygone years — the seat of
literature and science — to which memory will sometimes wander
back and linger around the scenes of other days and call
up the scarcely remembered features of classmates and teachers
yet the halls that resounded with the eloquence of declamation
the earnestness of debate and the more quiet recitation, and
the chapel that echoed the solemn voice of prayer — are
forever closed to me. The distant scenery was the haunt of
many a silent hour and as from the summit of the highest
hills in the background I was wont to survey the stunted pine and
oak forests interspersed with green fields — secluded hamlets
and wandering streams I would often indulge myself in a pleasing
reverie and as I meditated on the site of the ancient Council
fires of the Iroquois confederacy the halfconsumed coal and
brands of which still blacken the hill tops around the city
I could not forbear experiencing a sensation of sadness
at the ~~change~~ that equally awaits individuals as well as
nations — and which in some coming time may equally
befall our own happy land and the institution which
I have learned to call by the endearing name of Alma Mater

It is but justice to remark in relation to this picture that the terrace in front, the two buildings in the fore ground and the colonades extending back from them are the only portions of Union College yet built. The Chapel in the centre and the back buildings are yet to be erected.

(My room was in the left hand (North) college at the window marked with a dotted line and the letter A)

I have been boarding for the last week in the family of A C Van Dyke my nearest neighbor. at 12/ per week washing and mending included. I lodge at home and seldom stay in my boarding place except at meal times. I have not had much time to spend at home lately as it has been and is now quite sickly.

Sometimes I build a fire in my office and sit down to study my Medical works or to read your letters over.

None of my patients have died lately although several have been so sick — children especially that their lives were dispaired of. They are all convalescing.

No one but a physician can tell the heartfelt pleasure which is felt as at each succeeding visit the sufferer is found a little better. I believe the parents themselves cannot feel more pleased. I have seen within the last week many evidences which lead me to infer that I have secured and am increasing in the confidence of my employers. The anxious yet confiding appeal of the heart-stricken parent cannot fail to excite the sympathies and call forth the energies of the attending physician and I am frequently placed in situations where my responsibilities bear heavily on my shoulders and nothing but a confidence of ability and skill in the use of remedies could sustain me in the prosecution of my calling.

I derive daily more confidence in my own abilities and in the efficacy of my remedies and look forward to the time, dearest Mariah when I shall enjoy a reputation in my profession which shall extend beyond the precincts of my own town and vicinity and enjoy a competence for an old age, or for a day when I shall be unable to support myself and family by daily industry. At the age of thirty if life and health are spared to you and me I shall be free from debt and the owner of my home — with outstanding accounts besides, on interest, to the amount of several hundred dollars. In relation to our bridal dress, I am without any preferance or choice. Female dress is scarcely ever an object of notice or observation by me. I am perhaps too little particular about my own dress but must depend upon the taste and attentions of a wife for a suitable appearance. I ever strive to escape particular notice by having the fashion of my clothing no way remarkable either for the newness or oldness of its style. By following the medium I hope to pass without attracting observation or remark.

Respecting "the Day" I would propose Wednesday May Sixteenth, at 8 o'cl. A.M. so that we might reach home the same evening.

I have ever looked upon ostentation and parade at weddings as the height of folly particularly the long train of carriages which for miles will attract the attention of the inhabitants by exciting the remark — "Wonder who is married now?" Much pleasanter in my opinion would it be to ride off in a private carriage alone, attracting no attention and eliciting no remark. If I should express a wish in relation to the wedding it would be ~~that~~ the party invited should consist only of Relatives and the most intimate friends. I am not strenuous in these matters. If you have other preferances it will be my pleasure to favor them. I shall not rent my house to the man as I spoke of. Meanwhile I will whitewash and paint it within (and without perhaps) so that you can begin housekeeping without any previous trouble in cleaning &c. I will provide provisions of all kinds to be all ready by the time above refered to.

Would you have the knot tied by Mr Hurd? We want some one to do it strong. Meanwhile be assured that I remain as ever

Your affectionate Franklin.

Somerville N.J. Paid 5
March 20th 1849

James Kilham Esq
Irvin Lewis & Co
New York

H. 3

March 20. 1849.

VII.

Any different arrangements than those within which you may suggest will be adopted at once by me. The within remarks only apply to myself and contain my own views in relation to what I consider pleasant and suitable for such an occasion. P. B. K.

Turin March 26/49

Dearest Franklin

Your kind letter of the 20th I received on Thursday and being very busily engaged in work have delayed answering it until today. Being somewhat disappointed from having to stay at home from quarterly meeting on account of the rain I know of no better alternative than writing to the one I prize more highly than all earthly friends, for I deem such a friend one that sticketh closer than a brother and one for whom kind parents and the endearing ties that bind brother and sister are forsaken - - - yet how endearing may be a new relations when formed between two kindred minds, although in one sense built upon the ruins (or rather) from the ruins of childhood's happiest hours.

What can induce an affectionate sister, or kind brother to leave the home of his youth to spend a life with another, with all its changes but pure, and ennobling friendship? This alone induces me to leave home on Wednesday the 16th of May and hope I shall never have cause to regret the step.

Home how endearing that word; but alas! how soon may a change come over the homes of our infancy when the rude hand of death snatches one after another of its happy inmates.

How often do we experience feelings of sadness by being

so frequently admonished of the changes that not only await individuals and home, but nations and our own happy one must inevitably submit to the ravages of time, the ignorance of which, kind providence has kindly bestowed upon us and we should endeavor not to repine but be fortified for whatever awaits us.

Dearest Franklin the ________ hours we have spent so pleasantly furnish themes for reflection upon which I love to dwell particularly those spent in the school room when I was but a mere child then little did I think there ever would be an engagement existing between my teacher and myself had anyone told me so I should not have believed it. But what a change it is actually so and I am made to believe it though it seems more like a dream than reality.

In reference to our Wedding party it shall consist of none but relatives and a few friends and neighbors as we have thought of having a small company (choice and select). Do you think we could reach home the same evening at a season of the year when the roads are very rough generally in black river country. What think you the people of Somerville mistrust at your not renting your house to the tailor they must think something is to pay.

It is kept very still here yet; if Mrs. Woolworth knows anything about it I think she keeps it all to herself or it would get to me. How surprised the community will be, it will be like an electrical *shock to them (take them upon surprise) it will do one good; some one is asking me almost every day whether I am going to teach this summer or not (they suppose as a matter of course that I am) or if I have a school engaged? My answer is; not if Mary teaches as we can't both be spared.*

Last week I met with some communication from you (I suppose) in the Democrat over the signature FBH, and under the "Gold in Lewis Co.". I found it very interesting indeed, have heard several speak of the piece and wonder who wrote it, one says there is no one around here that can write like that. Shall I have the sincere pleasure of seeing you in April, or have you given up the idea of visiting Lewis Co. before May?

Devotedly, dearest Franklin

Your own Mariah

P.S. Do you know who has left your packages with me I should think it was not W. D. Yale though I dont know. Who did you send it by?

S. vulgaris
{common Lilac}

Somerville, March 29, 1849

Dearest Mariah. Your affectionate and very acceptable letter of the 26th just was received this morning and improve an early hour by answering it. How delightful is the task of spending a leisure hour in committing to paper the thoughts of the heart and the spirit,—who can sympathize with every sorrow and participate in every joyful hope and expectation of life.

The sickness here has subsided. One of my patients has died. There is not the slightest blame attached by any to me as his physician. This is the 1st death (except 2 cases of consumption) which has happened to me in Somerville.

Today I have been all day on a collecting tour to meet a payment of $160 due next week. By the loan of $100 from my brother I shall meet it. I (or we) own about $400 worth of land in Martinsburgh which I hope to sell. If so nothing will hinder me from swinging clear from debt speedily. How glorious it will feel to be out of debt! Then nothing will hinder us from enjoying life to our hearts content. I am probably worth about $1500 besides my debts. This does not include personal property or books, furniture, horse etc etc. Yet money is worth nothing except to the good we may derive from it. We must leave all behind us at the hour of death. The only motives which could actuate me in obtaining it would be—to live *respectably and easily—to supply needful nourishment for the mind and body—to lay aside a competence for old age or sickness—and to leave an inheritance which might be useful to posterity. I came home from my journey today sick with headache. The hirelings whom I pay for getting my meals sat a table as usual but earlier, and with nothing that I wanted. It is now 10 ocl. P.M.—6 hours since supper and I have a good appetite but no supper. If I was in my own house I could go to the pantry and help myself—or I could tell you that I was a little indisposed and you would prepare a little toast and a cup of tea for me even though it was not the regular time of supper.*

I think I have a little reason to think that the family where I board are a little penurious especially in setting a table but I say nothing and shall endure without a murmur—untill the 14 May next when I shall start for Turin. Were it not for the pleasing expectation of being soon a happy husband and provider for my own family I could not be happy for a moment. Do not infer from this letter that I am in a suffering condition—far from it. I am only just at this moment a little hungry,—have a little headache, and have lost my dinner.

I confide my troubles trivial as they are to a confidential friend knowing that tho small they will be appreciated and pitied.

The middle of May seems an age in the future. Yet two lunations will not have been completed before my pilgrimage as a single man—one blade of a pair of shears, will be ended and my happiness will be completed by becoming the devoted husband of a confiding and affectionate wife. My house now cheerless and tenantless except by myself during the lonely nights, will offer a cheerful welcome to the tired and weary owner.

Every day I count upon the time that must elapse and never did a schoolboy long for the last day of school when he might return home with more sincere desire than I do for the time to hasten when I shall have a home. You express a sensible regret upon leaving the home of your childhood. Yet it is but an exchange not an abandonment of home, and I trust that you will apply the sacred title home with far more sincerety and heartfelt pleasure to your residence in my house than the place of your nativity. You will feel a peculiar sensation new and strange as you sit down for the first time to the table spread by your own hand and in our own house by the side of your own husband—and as you look around the household which is henceforth to be managed and controlled by yourself an indescribable sensation of pleasure of responsibility and of hope will steal over you, and perhaps a tear mingled with a smile of mingled hope and trust, will steal upon you.

Our arrangements for reaching home the same evening will

depend upon the state of the roads. Sometimes they are dry and good at the season of the year.

The article signed F.B.H. was written by one Franklin B. Hough of the firm Hough and Kilham.

It is very doubtful about my coming to Turin before May.

The package was sent by a man who lived in Herkimer Co. with instruction to leave it at Mr. Yales or Van Name's Tavern at House-ville. W.D. Yale alone could know its destination. He probably sent it along to your house by some one who was passing having no knowledge of its contents. It is supposed generally here that I am to marry some one some where before long. No one asks any questions because they know that I know my own business. Perhaps I should tell them so if they asked me. Would you have the kindness to inquire of those who save their papers for no's 2, 3 and 4. vols of the Democrat. No. 3 I believe contains the President's Message. No. 2 and 4 contain some editorial articles from F.B.H. which I wish to preserve. I don't care about the no. that contains the Message.

Friday Morning, March 30. *This morning I am free from the pain in my head and feel as well as ever I did in my life. My remarks upon the boarding house I take back. They were written on an empty stomach. I did not know but that I should have to go to Ogdensburg on business next week but last night I received a letter which will remove anxiety about "the payment" and cause me no trouble.*

I have this morning been footing up my accounts—a full year having elapsed since my residence here.

During the year I have been absent to Champion many times, to Lewis County three or four times and to Canton once. The business losses by these journeys is probably about 50$. Besides, it has been a season of remarkable health. Yet my charges stand as follows—Good—$480.13 —Doubtful on which some if not all can be collected $158.75. Worthless, but which possibly may be got in something $73.66. Aggregate—$712.54. Many seasons afford double or even triple this amount. Yet even this exceeds the profits of a common dairy farmer. So you see we will be able to live comfortably and respectably if we enjoy good health, and without the toil and labor which agricultural business and the dairy impose upon the female members of a household.

Yet my time is not so much occupied but that I have a great deal to devote to reading and study. This time I principally devote to professional reading as I desire to excell in my business. Whether or not I succeed the future only will determine. I never get a new case without going to my books at the earliest moment of leisure and reading carefully every thing I find written concerning it.

This with constant reflection and careful observation will I hope improve my knowledge so as to enable me to detect early, decide correctly and treat successfully the numerous diseases and injuries to which humanity is subject.

Among the items of my collections this spring is a 5 gallon can full of nice clean maple molasses. They wanted to know what earthly use I could make of it. I replied that it is very useful in preparing syrups, etc. and in making pills. I might have added—to eat on buckwheat cakes.

I will endeavor to have all necessary provisions in readiness for the 16th of May and after. I have many debts which I have engaged to take in, grain, pork - ham - lard and other provisions.

Perhaps you may think the subjects of pork and lard rather ludicrous along side with protestations of love and the sublimities of true friendship. Yet, bread and love have a remote relation because the later would die without the former and protestations of friendship and affections from a husband and a provider without the aliment needful for the body would be rather poetical than practical and would do to go with fiction and romance rather than with the realities of life.

With the sentiments of devoted affection I remain

Sincerely your own Franklin.

Turin, April 3rd, 1849

Dearest Franklin,

Your kind letter of the 29th received yesterday and will hasten this pleasant evening, to answer it that you may not be disappointed, in its reception at an early hour. "How delightful indeed is the task" of spending a part of our time in communicating to each other our thoughts and wishes of the heart, where we know this affection is reciprocated.

I am happy to hear that you are prospering in your business, and that no more of your patients have died. I think that F. B. Hough must be a very skillful physician, if he has as difficult cases to attend to as they have in this community, and loose no more patients than he does. What think you? I think his skill must exceed that of Mr. C of our town, for I am sure they loose an average, one a month, and perhaps more. You will pardon me for extolling <u>that physician</u> as he is the one that we have been pretty well acquianted with, for several years, and expect I shall become better able to alleviate some of the misfortunes, and sufferings, to which he is exposed, ere long, than I am at the present, such as procuring meals at an unreasonable hour for the <u>long wished</u> for Franklin at his return from a long and tedious tour, with many "trivial" acts which should be performed by the wife. Did I say wife? - - -

I think that term should be applied to persons older than myself and those better prepared for so responsible a position, for I have ever thought she had much to do, to increase the happiness of the domestic circle whose joys are never known beyond its limits. This impression was never more forcible than whilst teaching and boarding in different families when I had a fine time to witness some striking contrasts in their enjoyments and I formed a resolution then should I ever become a wife I would do all that I was capable of doing to render life useful and agreeable, little did I think that my welfare was so closely connected with your own, or so soon be reminded of any resolutions. As the bell is ringing it reminds me of retiring and I must bid goodnight, without love's evermost token, hoping that you are free from the headache.

Wednesday Evening

After having rested sweetly I resume writing for I know of nothing more pleasing than to converse with a dear friend this pleasant and lovely morning. All is still and serene nothing (save the music of the birds) to disturb the quiet that reigns around me.

Creation thus at rest fills the mind with a solemn awe, and speaks to it of the omnipresence of the Creator. Each chord of my heart seems to vibrate responsive to nature's music, which I do so much admire yes I am a passionate lover of nature. I love to wander in the lone woods, linger by the murmuring streams, and listen to the music of the distant cascade; but how much may be added to such pleasures, by knowing that we have a friend that can appreciate these beauties.

I have had several applications to teach this spring, but no one will give me my price. There is a great excitement produced by my not taking a school but they will probably find out the reason six weeks from today if not before - - - We are going to have a school at the village taught by Miss Sykie a sister of the last winter principal. She thinks of boarding with your sister (Mrs. Woolworth). Lavantia thinks of taking music lessons if she brings a pianno. I am pleased to hear that you have procured a can of nice maple molasses, and I guess it will not all be made into syrups and pills for I can find better use for it than that, then we will save Mrs. VanDyke the pleasure of exhibiting her penuriousness. As for our furniture it is not all ready yet though I expect it will be in time. If I have leisure I intend to make the carpets whilst here that I may have help.

Please accept these hastily written lines with the assurance that I am your friend as ever.

Mariah

Lonicera Hirsuta
{Hairy Honeysuckle}

Somerville (Rossie) April 7, 1849

Your acceptable letter has been received and I improve the first leisure moment in answering. I have had more leisure within a few days which I have improved in sawing wood and piling it up today in my wood house—for summer use. Geo. Green formerly of Turin, has been quite sick but is better and begins to go out. I have a patient 8 miles from here beyond Gouverneur village whom I am to see today. So you see I have a reputation that extends out of my circuit of business in one direction at least. There are 3 doctors in Gouverneur village.

You speak of your age as very unusual in a wife. If you look around you, you will find that a majority of your associates who have married did so before they were as old as yourself.

There is a man among my customers, here, who married a woman (?) who is 11 years old. This is ridiculous I must admit. Often did he have to call her home from play with other children to get his dinner and once he is said to have applied the "sprouts" (for shame) for the fault of getting a chicken "drunk" by placing its head under its wing and whirling it around.

There is reason in all things but I think that you will not be deviating from the beaten track—or give occasion for remarks—or occasion the smallest degree of gossip by engaging in matrimony at your age. My sister Mrs. Smith of Gouverneur suspects me very strongly of corresponding with some one by the name of Kilham, but cannot make out for certain. I asked her the other day if she was making calculations for going out to Lewis Co. in May next—about the 16th. She said she thought likely if I would tell her for certain who and where and when. This I of course declined.

I intend to go out to Champion next week to see my darling child. How tender is the relation between parent and child! It would break my heart if she should sicken and die. Yet I see children of her age and people of every age and condition of life who are taken away by slow and insidious, or painful and violent sickness—or destroyed by accident. None but a father can sympathize with a parents anxieties, and as I have been called to minister to sick children, I realize the anxieties of the parents by placing myself in their relation. I am thus incited to the performance of my official duty with zeal and earnestness, and when successful feel very grateful.

I contemplate making certain changes in the arrangement of my house but will not do so untill you can be consulted as a wife. It will be the greatest pleasure to listen to your suggestions and conform to your wishes.

Solomon Pratt is about erecting a store within 20 feet of my house which will obstruct the prospect some but not impair the light.

As for the prospect it matters but little as all the windows on the side towards his store are in the summer season shaded by vines. One thing is certain that the pleasantest room in the house—the parlor can never have its prospect lessened. The front windows look out on little piazza and yard planted with lilac and rose bushes, peonies and lilies. I have three maple trees and two Balm of Gilead trees in full operation before my house. The latter are very thrifty. The maples have been planted a year and are thriving. In my rambles last summer I found a specimen of Lonicera hirsuta (very rare) which I have planted before my piazza. It is living and will be very ornamental. When I came from Ohio I brought slips of the Rosa Eglantine, a climbing rose which I will bring from Champion and plant in the little yard this spring. It twines everywhere, climbs trees and poles and bears clumps of single roses very fragrant.

I have seen white and ornamental varieties engrafted upon this and in blossom around the chamber windows of houses.

But above all I delight in collecting and studying wild flowers from the forests or margin of lakes and prescipes.

Among the most pleasant of my anticipations is this—that I shall have a bosom companion who will sympathize with me in these studies and share in my pleasure derived from the study and analysis of these beautiful productions. Although my territorial limits are narrow, yet the world is mine. So far as the beauties of nature are concerned and it matters not who holds the deed of the soil so long as the pleasant woodlands, green meadows, and wandering streams lie open to my sight inviting my admiration and lifting the grateful heart in adoration to the benevolent giver of blessings and creator of so many beauties.

Mr. Armstrong the principal of the Goverenur Seminary invited me to prepare for publication a catalogue of St. Lawrence county plants for publication like that of Lewis County. My opportunities for rambling in the forest are at an end and I am unable to procure the requisite data without assistance from other enthusiastic collectors. Possibly I may teach a class in Botany at Goverenur this summer giving 1 lesson a week. If so the students would bring me the specimens of "indiginous" flowers necessary for such an undertaking.

You will be delighted with the appearance of Mr. Armstrong the principal of the Goverenur School. I shall invite him to visit me perhaps spend a day or two with me. He is passionately fond of music especially the Guitar—is an elegant landscape painter, and thoroughly versed in all the sciences. We are kindred spirits. My greatest trouble is the probability that he will leave Goverenur this summer for Cayuga Co. where he once lived. They offer him very strong inducements.

A newspaper, the "Northern New Yorker" is soon to be started at Governeur. I expect to make some arrangement for furnishing something for its columns statedly. Writing for the press has ever been with me a favorite business. Profitless thus far but very pleasant. I delight to sign my pieces with some fictitious name, and hear the people guess who is the author. Get if you can the Democrat for April 3. It has not reached me and I want to complete my files. You need not send it to me but lay it by. Another summer (1 year *+) there will be a plank road from here to Turin when the journey would not be so much dreaded. I trust the roads will be good on the 16th. They are dry and quite good here now. I have not had a fire in the house for several weeks. I stay in my office most of the time till late evening and then crawl into my bed—(without making it) and sleep till morning. Mrs. Van Dyke makes the bed twice or three times a week only. They are well meaning folks but have always been accustomed to live cheaply and dont realize how it seems or looks to set a poor table. Yet about 40 days longer and I set down at my own table spread to my own liking.*

Meanwhile be assured that the day seems distant and the hours drag their slow weary lengths along that separate me from <u>you</u>, that will transform me from a lonely friendless (so far as feelings go) Man —into an affectionate and happy <u>husband</u>.

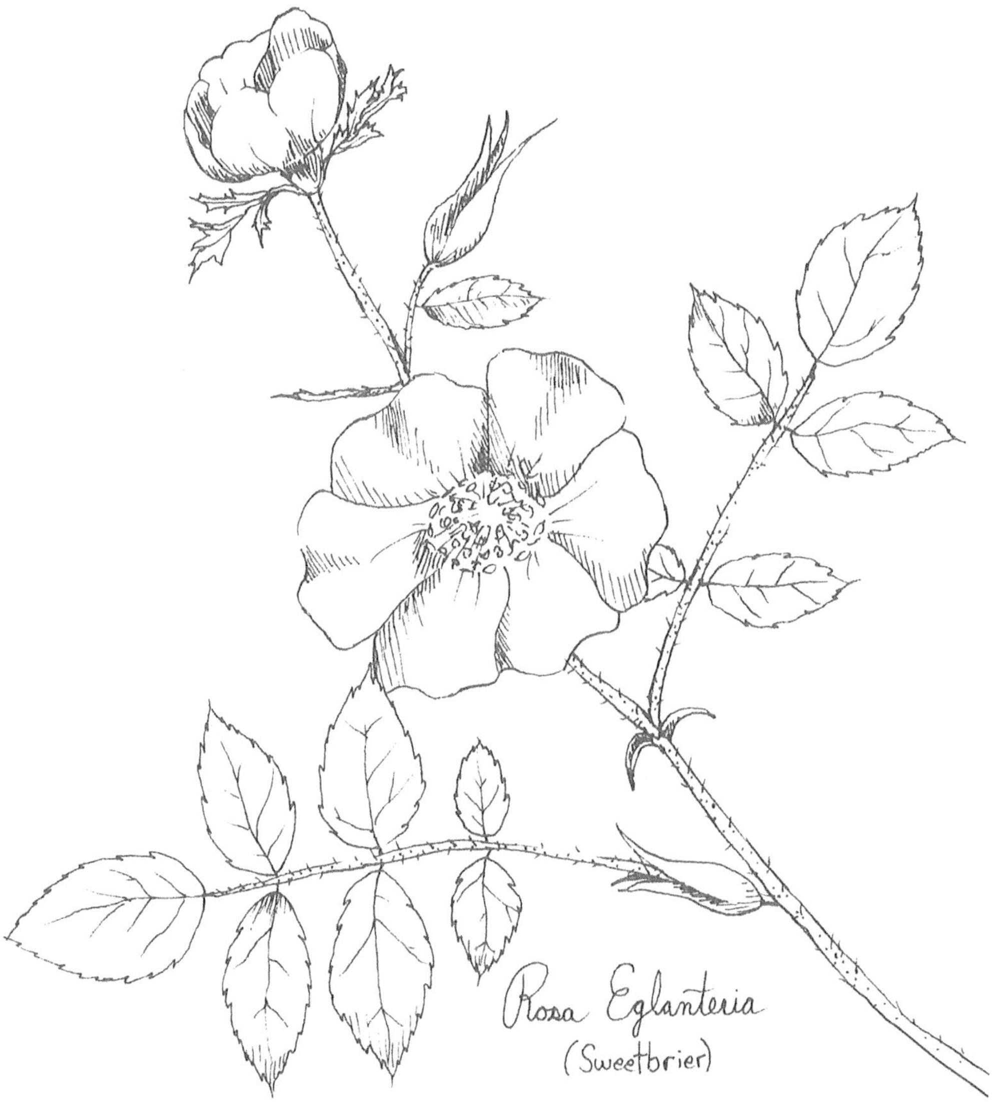
Rosa Eglanteria
(Sweetbrier)

Turin April 15th/49

Dearest Franklin

Unavoidable attention to my work has thus far (from Tuesday until now) prevented me from answering your kind letter though think not it the result of negligence, for nothing would afford more pleasure than writing immediately if my time would allow it. I am pleased to hear that you have been so successful in your business (to cure up all sickness) I think your reputation extends in more than one direction; it will ere long in every direction. Where do we find one that will not if he has a near and dear friend sick send for the most skillful physician, if he is many miles away. You, without doubt belong to the above named class, then why should your reputation not extend all ways? Think me not a flatterer for flattery I despise.

I am sorry to hear that Mr. Pratt is erecting a building to hid the prospect of your house though I presume it will make but little difference whilst the windows are shaded with vine.

I have been expecting you here for about a week for I thought if you visited Champion you would of course visit Turin though have given up the idea now. Did you have a pleasant visit, and find Lora Maria well? I suppose you obtained the plant you spoke of and have it now planted at home.

You say that your sister Mrs. Smith suspects you of cor-

responding with some one by the name of Kilham how did she find it out? But we know such news will get out some way or other if any thing will.

I dont think either of my brothers could correspond with a lady long and I not know it. The news begins to get around here. I hear it hinted by one or two I cant get them to tell me who his name is they think they will wait until they are sure of its being so, that it may not be a false rumor. I hope they will wait until they are sure enough before they let me know his name then perhaps I shall know it as well as they, what think you? Cousin Leonard C. Kilham told me yesterday that he heard I was going to be married to F. B. Hough, said that one of your best friends told him so and would not let me know who he was. I was very anxious to know that I might tell you. I wondered how such a story could be started. I entreated of him not to say any thing about it for fear that Mr. Hough would hear of the trash and take it as an imposition. He thought I must be trying to blind his eyes for he heard a pretty strait story, and from that said it must be so. I asked him how long before it was to happen said this person told him in about six weeks but he thought not in less than six months. Well said I, it is well that I have heard of it that I may commence making preparations if I am going to leave so soon.

The paper you spoke of I have in reserve and will keep it for you. I have not as yet obtained those numbers of the Democrat you alluded to, have spoken to several that take the papers and have not saved them I presume I shall be able to get them of some one. It is quite wintry here now, instead of dust that we have had for several weeks past we have snow the ground is covered so that sleighing is quite passable on the plank road. I hope it will not last long for it is too near the 16th of May. Do you know how many of your friends and who will be here to the Wedding if so please write as I would like to know before making preperations for the company. E. R. Collins told me the other day she should have to learn the nuptial quick step to play for me the 4th of July so you see by that she mistrusts something. What time and day do you intend to arrive here? Please excuse this hastily written letter and accept it from your sincere and affectionate

Mariah

Old Mr. Eli Rogers was buried yesterday he died very suddenly was sick but a day or two.

Somerville, April 21, 1849

Dearest Mariah, *Since receiving your last I have visited Champion circumstances having hindered me from going sooner. I found my child well. She talks about me every day, they say. The family evince for me the same anxiety and regard that they did while my first wife was alive, and on my going away Mrs. E. came and stuffed 3 pairs of new woolen socks into my pocket saying they would save me from paying money for them and that she had knit them on purpose for me. On my return I stopped and surveyed some Indian forts in Leray. I intend to send the maps and description to Albany to the Regents where they will be published at the state's expense. I procured stone pipes, stone chisels, fragments of pottery from the grounds.*

Pratt's store is raised. It does not look so near as I expected and I have no reason to murmur.

I intend to start from here for Turin early on the 14th arriving at Mr. Arthurs the same evening. On the 15th in the forenoon I hope to see you. Probably I shall go to Turin Village in the p.m. On Wednesday morning we shall stand up and promise, and the same day start for home getting to Denmark, Carthage, Antwerp or Somerville as the roads may happen to be. Have you anything to suggest in relation to this arrangement? If so I will with sincere pleasure con-

form to it. Shall we marry on the 15th in the evening, so as to start early the next morning and be sure of getting through in one day? How would this plan please you? In relation to the guests whom I intend to "warn out" to attend the wedding I would say that I should be glad to invite my mother, W. Arthur, his wife, daughter and 3 boys, Horatio H. and wife, Mr. Woolworth's family and P. B. Yale and family. It will give me pleasure to meet as many of your friends as you may see proper to invite. I presume that your relatives are so numerous that none but such will be invited. There is danger of giving offence where we begin to invite acquaintances for nobody knows when or where to stop. I speak of these things merely as suggestions,—not that I expect or wish you to be influenced by them. It rather seems that it will be better to have the ceremony come off on the 15th (eve) as there will be more time to spend with the company. I have no choice besides for I consider myself sure of your hand and heart and your lasting affection which 12 hours difference will not affect or lessen. I will not write to Mr. Hurd or to say of my expected guests until I receive your answer.

I am disappointed in getting slips from that rose as it has not sprouted and I can get no slips having roots.

In a year or two there will be plenty of them. Perhaps it may please you to learn that little Lora M (2½ years old) has learned without instruction all her letters—that she takes more pleasure in printed letters than most children do in pictures and that her whole soul is bent upon learning to read so that they endeavor to direct her mind by toys and playthings from her paper. I think she will never remember the time when she could not read. Her health is remarkably good.

As I have to go this morning to attend to a distant call I shall have for the want of time bring this letter to a close. Be assured dearest Mariah that it is not for lack of anything to say or write, for I could write ever many sheets without fatigue or weariness.

Rest assured of my continuous and perpetual love

And believe me

your <u>own</u> Franklin.

Turin, April 24th 1849

Dearest Franklin,

Your letter of the 21st I have just received and hasten to answer it that we may know for certain the day (or evening) the wedding is to go off. I think it will be much pleasanter in the evening for if it is in the morning we shall have to have the company in short order, (so we say evening).

I prefer the one of the 16th if it will make no difference with you, our people likewise think it better be at 8 o'clock P.M. on Wednesday as we shall have so much to accomplish that week before Wednesday. You will of course leave your place on Monday if it is not before the evening of the 16th, unless you do your visit will be rather short in Turin.

Will it not be soon enough to invite the guests on the 12th of May if the invitations are given out before that I am afraid it will be all over town before hand; it is kept very still here but very few have heard of it yet. I am not going to write to my friends before Monday the 14th. How surprized they will be. Those that have heard of it say they dont believe it. I had not thought of inviting any uncles and aunts none of my relatives but cousins; though perhaps I may.

Doctor Tracy of Collinsville has been lately married to an acquaintance of mine Miss Jane Chittenden of Mount Pleasant

Wayne County, Penn. She is not 18 yet (very young). She use to live with her sister at Collinsville where he became acquainted with her. You did not mention your sister Mrs. Smith's name as one of the guests is she not coming, if so, why not?

What think you Lora would say at your miniature—which I so often look at—if she could but see it? I wish I could show it to her. I rather think she would know it, it is so natural. I dont know but it will excite the Methodists some our employing Mr. Hurd but I cant help that for I would rather have a Justice officiate than the Methodist minister we have on our circuit this year.

Please pardon me for the shortness of this epistle as I am now interrupted with company and must close. Will you please answer this as soon as convenient that I may know if you agree with us on the evening of the 16th.

As ever your affectionate

Mariah

Somerville, April 25, 1849 (Wednes Evening)

Dearest Mariah, *Your letter of yesterday was received today. It will be my greatest pleasure to assent to the time and hour of marriage which you propose. I will start from here on Monday morning as I first proposed.*

Today I have been making soap. They ask what I want of soap? I tell them it is to save my materials. <u>We</u> have about ½ a barrel full (to begin the world with). Although a raw hand at the business I have had the best of success and shall know later how to proceed another time if my assistence can be useful.

The kettle set in an arch is a most valuable contrivence for this business; for washing etc. Some of the neighbors solicit the privilege of using it every year for this business.

Tomorrow I shall devote to whitewashing having procured lime today.

You ask if Mrs. Smith is not intending to attend. She has had an invitation to go somewhere she knows not where on the 16th of May but thinks it out of the question <u>to take</u> much less to <u>leave</u> her children.

I have as strong a dislike for the Methodist preacher of Turin as yourself. Who cares for what the Methodists will say or think? In such matters I would wish to consult no other persons preferences than our own.

It is generally expected here that I marry some one in Turin before long. My letters are mailed without reserve and they all go to Turin. Of course this gives them reason to suspect the case but the when and who are mysterious.

The spring has begun to open by the opening of the vernal flowers and my pleasure from this source would be very much enhanced could I share with you the satisfaction of collecting and studying them. The Hepatica, the Claytonia, the Dicentra and the Trillium are among the daily objects of my observation besides great numbers of our forest trees. More than twenty species of plants have been observed in bloom this spring at this place. I have frequent opportunities of rambling in the woods on my errands of mercy to the sick and I prize exceedingly these chances of studying nature.

The new moon just trembling on the horizon reminds me it will not have waned before our hearts and hands will be united forever! As we watch night to night its eastern progress among the constellations we shall be reminded of the approach of our happiness, and when as its full orb shall rise in the east, as the sun disappears, our union will be delayed but a single week. Although we may be frequently wishing different periods of time at our end, how short and fleeting do they appear when we contemplate them in the retrospect! The orb of night as it waxes and wanes is a fit emblem of the changing scenes of earth and the rise and fall of the destiny of nations.

May it not prove an emblem of our affection, which like the steady polestar should shine with a steady serene and constant glow of love, and mutual tenderness and regard, suffering no obscuration, never deceiving, but always maintaining a constancy and uniformity, unaffected by changes—undiminished by time.

At the longest, but comparatively a few moons and our union will be sundered by death. We are neither of us sure of attaining the 70 years allotted to man.

Accidents and disease remove the fondest companion, from the tenderest embraces, and we have no assurance that such will not be our lot.

Yet hope the lamp of life, pictures to us a long, a busy, a useful, and happy future,—when after having shared the joys and divided the sorrows of life's pilgrimage, we shall feel like the tired travelers, the necessity of repose. When having encountered the cares of a lifetime and the labor which the God of nature has imposed upon us, we shall sleep with our fathers.

That a long and happy life, with many of the roses, and few of the thorns, which beset the pilgrim's fathers may be ours, is the sincere wish of your own intended husband and true friend.

Franklin.

Turin, April 29, 1849

Dearest Franklin

Supposing of course you would like to hear again from your friend M, I will donate a few moments in writing to you. I received your last in due time, for which I am very thankful, and by reading it over was a reminder of past scenes which furnish subjects for many pleasant thoughts. Scenes which will never be forgotten as long as memory lasts.

And shall we not in future times look back to these days as bright spots in our existence? or shall there be other spots that will outshine these, other scenes of greater enjoyment which will eclips these, I hope the chords of affection that bind us together shall ever grow stronger and we become more and more attached to each other as long as we live. And why should we not so long as we place in each other that entire confidence we are accustomed to? Can it be possible this confidence shall ever be lessened, or anything happen which shall diminish our love for each other. Let us never harbor such a thought, but guard well this plant that it may ever increase.

Tuesday morn

With a beautiful May morning sad remembrance of the past presents itself. The departure of friends!

Nearly two years have passed since the death of a beloved Father and lovely Sister. We can no longer extend to them the greeting hand or join with that sister in singing the cheerful song, but the white bosomed marble points to the place of their peaceful repose. Pamelia's voice has ceased its melody on earth, but she has now a seraphs lyre and she breathes from her harp, music untainted by anything mortal. I'll think of her not as in the grave, but a pure spirit in the regions of bliss.

In thinking of friends that have been taken from us let us not forget those we have and whose society we can enjoy.

How grateful ought we to be for present enjoyments. One parent is gone yet I have one left a dear kind mother and I will not murmur though it is right to mourn for departed friends. Our Savior wept, then let the hallowed tears of affection moisten their graves, but we will endeavor not to repine, but submit to the Disposer of all events.

I suppose I shall see you here two weeks from this morning how pleasing the thought. Is it possible 3 months have passed since I last saw you? "Yes how fleeting is the time when viewed in retrospect"?

My work flies about as fast as time I

am very busy dont get time for much of anything but work.

How did you get along whitewashing and how did you like the business as well as making soap I presume. Excuse the shortness of this epistle and accept it from your true and affectionate friend

Mariah

Please write as soon as convenient for nothing affords more pleasure than reading one of your good long letters.

Somerville, St. Lawrence Co. May 4, 1849

Dearest Mariah.

I improve an early opportunity in answering your letter of Tuesday. Ere two weeks shall have elapsed we shall be pleasantly settled at housekeeping,—happy in our mutual love—and happy in the confidence of an agreeable future. I have good success in whitewashing, soap boiling, house cleaning, etc and think this my first apprenticeship may be of future service. It will be a great pleasure to lend a helping hand in these little domestic labors.

Today I have plowed my garden, and tomorrow I shall plan to plant and make my lettuce and onion beds. This week I got three bushels of wheat ground and during the coming week will make arrangements for a supply of butter, lard, potatoes, etc without which "affection" could not long subsist. With these little helps I hope to begin housekeeping under pleasant circumstances and doubt not our happiness will long endure.

Mrs. Van Dycke has today volunteered her assistance in washing floors—business which I know nothing about—for which she is to have use of my kettle and arch etc etc.

My little yard begins to look fresh with greenness at the approach of spring. Some Daffodils (narcissus pseudonarcissas) which I planted last spring are in full bloom—and I have transplanted them in many places. I hope by the 17th or 18th the lilacs will be in bloom—it will look so pleasant, and they will seem decked out in an especial manner to welcome their future mistress. You can but partly realize the impatience with which I look forward to the time when I shall be settled in a home of my own—be seated at my own table and enjoy the confidence and affection of my own wife. The other night when I came home from a fatiguing ride and went to bed supperless (Mr. VD's people had gone to bed) I dreamed that as I entered my house you came to meet me—kissed me affectionately—and anxiously enquired if I had been to supper. Yet how delusive is a dream! In the morning when I awoke to the consciousness that although I owned a house, I was homeless, and my feelings reminded me that I needed food. Mr. Van Dycke's people are very kind hearted and do all they can—so far as they know how to make me confortable. Mrs. VD has occasionally made up my bed, although that was not specified in the bargain. But another week and a day, and I shall be on my way to meet the dearest object of my heart. But another fortnight and I shall be the happy husband of an affectionate wife.

The time will elapse before one can realize it and the first thing that we shall read in the county papers as we look at the department headed "Marriages" will be the following.—

"Married in Turin on the 16th Inst by the Rev. N. Hurd

Franklin B. Hough M.D. of Somerville, St. Lawrence County to Miss Mariah Kilham of the former place."

Friends will stare at it if it has not come to their ears before and wonder they did not know it beforehand,—and strangers will glance at the announcement with indifferance or perhaps casually ask who are the parties. In a few weeks it will be forgotten and yourself will only be known or designated as Mrs. Hough, or Dr. Hough's wife of Somerville.

Yet the occurence will not thus vanish from the recollection of the parties. The 16th of May will long be mentioned as a happy anniversary. Your name although changed will not lessen the familiarity of your paternal name or diminish the warmth of the affection you bear towards those whose name will still be Kilham. Nor should it. The early attachments of families should be long cherished with the same tender regard as in the years of youth and childhood when the family circle embraced its members in a common interest— a common cause and rendered the sacred name of home synonimous with that of World.

Alas, how many have to reverse these terms and call the World their home. How thankful we should be that we have a pleasant and convenient spot which we can make a pleasant paradise by our mutual endeavor. In 1844 when travelling I visited the falls of

Niagara. Spell bound I lingered for several days around these aweful and majestic waters and sought from every propect a view of this awe inspiring wonder of the world. Visitors are requested as they cross the bridge to the Island to write in a book their name, residence and destination. In chancing to look back along the names, my eye fell upon that of one with which I was familiar by reputation—that of Francis Abbott "the hermit of the falls". He labored under a gentle form of delirium and in his wanderings he came to this place. Naturally endowed with an exquisite love of the sublimities of nature his soul was entranced with the scene and he lived a hermit's life on the Island for many months until at length he was accidentally drowned. In the book above mentioned he had written his residence "the World"—his destination "the Grave". Few can say more. None can say less. If then life is so brief a span and the grave inevitably opens sooner or later to receive us, ought we not to endeavor by all that in us lays to mitigate each other's sorrows, to drop the tear of sympathy over the misfortunes, to throw the mantle of charity over the shortcomings and the errors of the life as well as shed the tear of sorrow over the grave of those we love? That you will see in me faults is not less than you can expect—for the mortal is perfect? I trust a spirit of kindness and regard will lead you to forgive and gently reprove whatever you see amiss that I may more and more deserve your affection.

I shall not write to Mr. Hurd or any one else. When I come out I shall have sufficient time to attend to all such business and invite all the friends I wish to have present—among my relations.

I inclose in this wrapper a letter to Lake of the Democrat. I wish you would let Geo. or some one else hand it to him. I sent it in this letter to save him the postage. He need not know of course how it came or to whom it was sent.

This will be the last of my letters to you before I have an opportunity of communicating personally whatever I have to say.

The time is so brief I shall not expect to hear from you again unless you have something special to write. It might by some little delay or accident not reach me until after I have started.

Meanwhile be assured that you are ever present in my thoughts and that the brief period of our separation will seem an age. Be assured that my affection will not change with the nuptial ceremony but will remain for years undiminished by time, or condition or circumstances, but that ever, as now, I shall always remain,

Your true friend, and affectionate lover

Franklin

Postscript

From the diary of Franklin B. Hough, March 25, 1848 - Jan 13, 1852*

Saturday, 12 May Started early for Turin. Rode in rain part of the P.M. Stopped at Lewis' and Carthage. Spent the night at W. Arthur's. Went on east road.
Tuesday, 15 Went to Turin in A.M. Spent P.M. at Mrs. Kilham's. Sat up till late.
Wednesday 16th May, 1849. Spent the day at Mrs. Kilham's. Was married in the evening by Rev. N. Hurd to Mariah E., second daughter of the late Heman Kilham. Party not very large. Every circumstance and incident pleasant.
Thurs. 17 May. Started in morning with wife. Arrived at S. Lewis' Tavern before sunset where we spent the night.
Fri. 18 Arrived home about noon. Spent P.M. in arranging and fixing up about house.

* The early diaries of Franklin G. Hough are in the possession of the Lewis County Historical Society Museum, Lyons Falls, New York.